HAMMOND

STUDENT
WORLD
ATLAS

CONTENTS

THE WORLD AND ITS REGIONS

MAPS OF THE WORLD

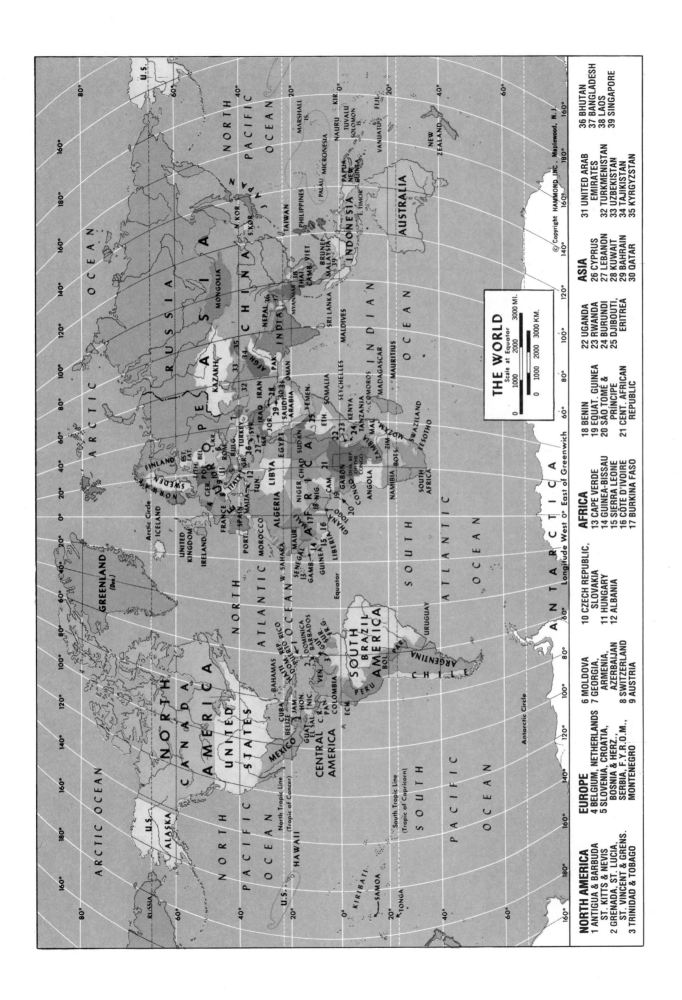

THE WORLD

Scale at Equator

1000   2000   3000 MI.

0   1000   2000   3000 KM.

Longitude West 0° East of Greenwich

NORTH AMERICA
1 ANTIGUA & BARBUDA
  ST. KITTS & NEVIS
2 GRENADA, ST. LUCIA,
  ST. VINCENT & GRENS.
3 TRINIDAD & TOBAGO

EUROPE
4 BELGIUM, NETHERLANDS
5 SLOVENIA, CROATIA,
  BOSNIA & HERZ.,
  SERBIA, F.Y.R.O.M.,
  MONTENEGRO
6 MOLDOVA
7 GEORGIA,
  ARMENIA,
  AZERBAIJAN
8 SWITZERLAND
9 AUSTRIA
10 CZECH REPUBLIC,
   SLOVAKIA
11 HUNGARY
12 ALBANIA

AFRICA
13 CAPE VERDE
14 GUINEA-BISSAU
15 SIERRA LEONE
16 CÔTE D'IVOIRE
17 BURKINA FASO
18 BENIN
19 EQUAT. GUINEA
20 SÃO TOMÉ &
   PRÍNCIPE
21 CENT. AFRICAN
   REPUBLIC
22 UGANDA
23 RWANDA
24 BURUNDI
25 DJIBOUTI,
   ERITREA

ASIA
26 CYPRUS
27 LEBANON
28 KUWAIT
29 BAHRAIN
30 QATAR
31 UNITED ARAB
   EMIRATES
32 TURKMENISTAN
33 UZBEKISTAN
34 TAJIKISTAN
35 KYRGYZSTAN
36 BHUTAN
37 BANGLADESH
38 LAOS
39 SINGAPORE

© Copyright HAMMOND INC., Maplewood, N.J.

3

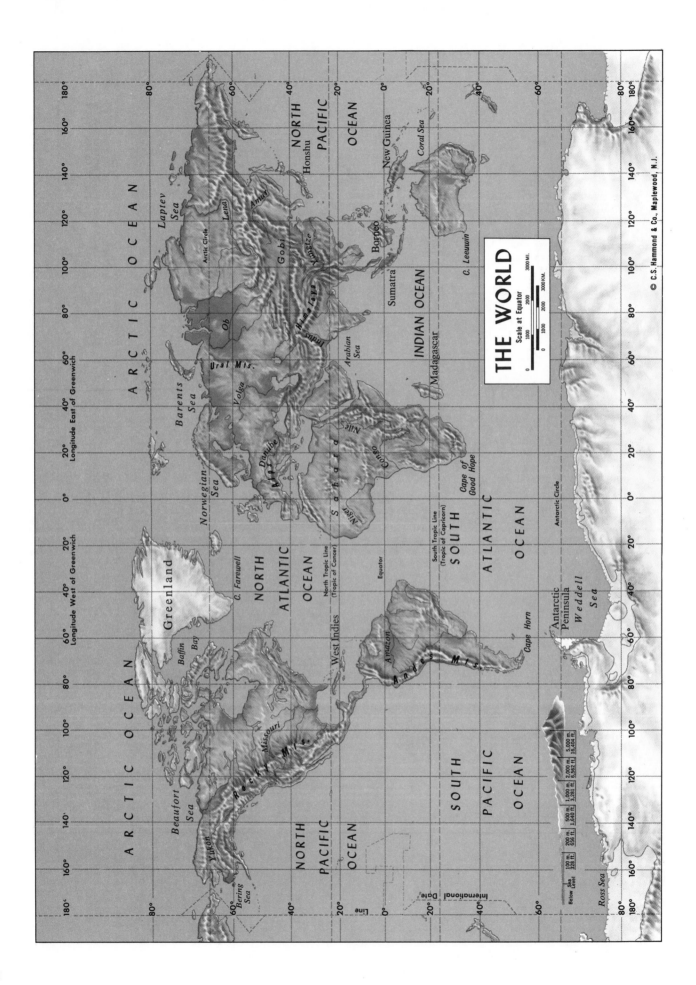

THE WORLD

Scale at Equator

1000   2000   3000 MI.

1000   2000   3000 KM.

© C.S. Hammond & Co., Maplewood, N.J.

ARCTIC OCEAN

NORTH PACIFIC OCEAN

Honshu

New Guinea

Coral Sea

Laptev Sea

Lena

Anadir

Gobi

Yangtze

Himalaya

Indus

Ob

Ural Mts.

Volga

Barents Sea

Arctic Circle

Borneo

Sumatra

INDIAN OCEAN

Madagascar

C. Leeuwin

Arabian Sea

Nile

Congo

Sahara

Niger

Danube

Alps

Norwegian Sea

Cape of Good Hope

SOUTH ATLANTIC OCEAN

South Tropic Line (Tropic of Capricorn)

North Tropic Line (Tropic of Cancer)

Equator

C. Farewell

NORTH ATLANTIC OCEAN

West Indies

Greenland

Baffin Bay

Amazon

Andes Mts.

Cape Horn

Antarctic Peninsula

Weddell Sea

Antarctic Circle

Longitude East of Greenwich

Longitude West of Greenwich

Missouri

Rocky Mts.

Yukon

Beaufort Sea

Bering Sea

NORTH PACIFIC OCEAN

SOUTH PACIFIC OCEAN

International Date Line

Ross Sea

ARCTIC OCEAN

Below Sea Level   100 m. 328 ft.   200 m. 656 ft.   500 m. 1,640 ft.   1,000 m. 3,281 ft.   2,000 m. 6,562 ft.   5,000 m. 16,404 ft.

180° 160° 140° 120° 100° 80° 60° 40° 20° 0° 20° 40° 60° 80° 180° 160°

4

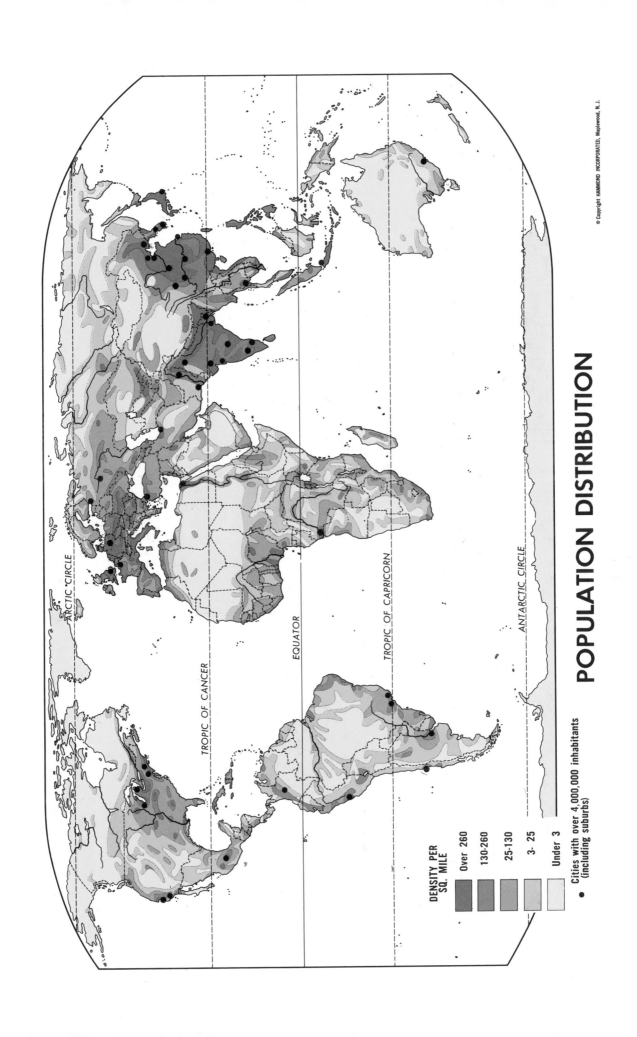

POPULATION DISTRIBUTION

DENSITY PER
SQ. MILE

Over 260
130-260
25-130
3- 25
Under 3

• Cities with over 4,000,000 inhabitants
  (including suburbs)

ARCTIC CIRCLE

TROPIC OF CANCER

EQUATOR

TROPIC OF CAPRICORN

ANTARCTIC CIRCLE

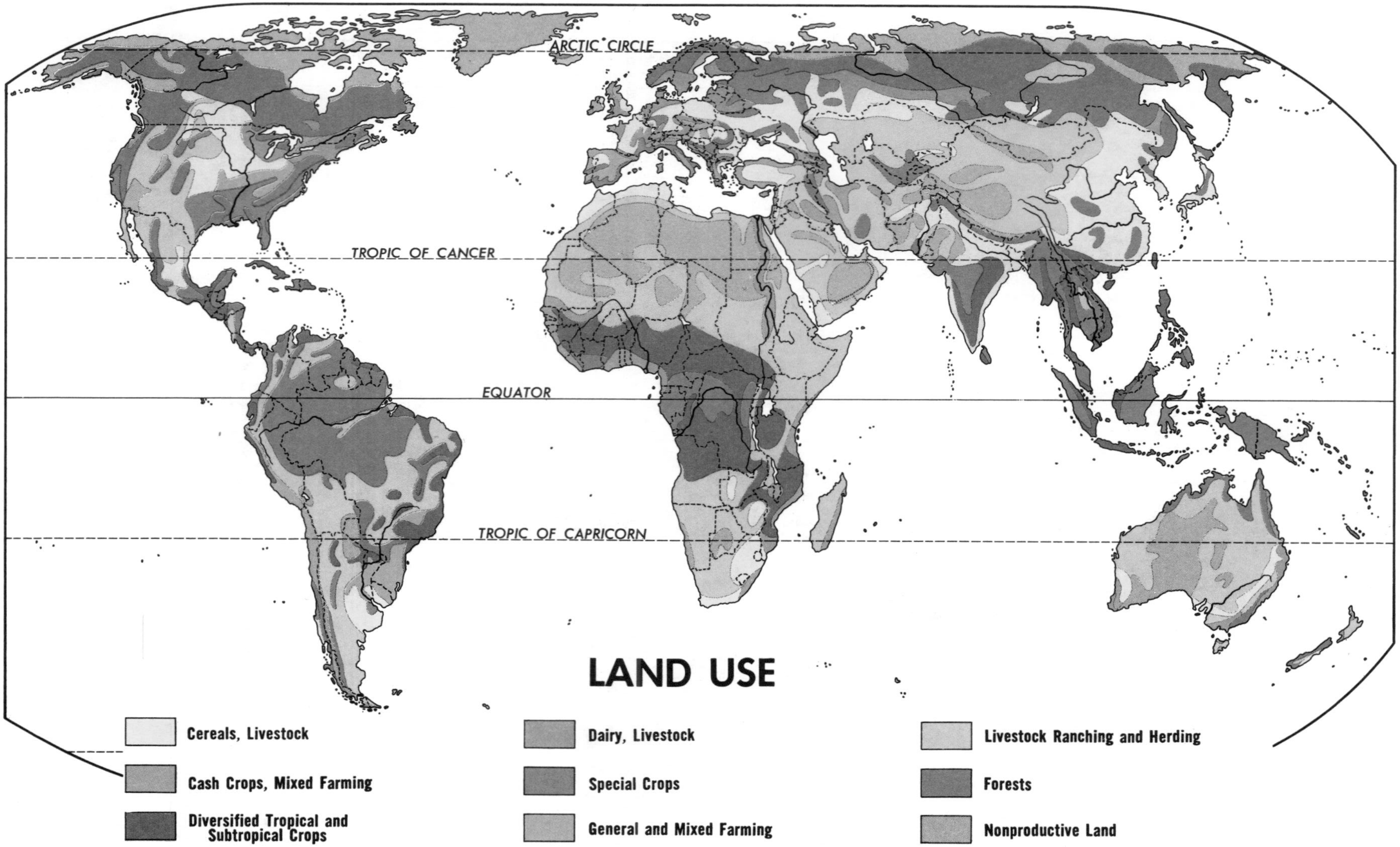

LAND USE

ARCTIC CIRCLE

TROPIC OF CANCER

EQUATOR

TROPIC OF CAPRICORN

Cereals, Livestock

Cash Crops, Mixed Farming

Diversified Tropical and Subtropical Crops

Dairy, Livestock

Special Crops

General and Mixed Farming

Livestock Ranching and Herding

Forests

Nonproductive Land

THE WORLD

The earth is our world. It gives us everything we need to live. Yet it is a very small place. The third planet from the sun, the earth is only the fifth largest of the solar system's nine planets in size. The diameter of the earth is about 8,000 miles (13,000 kilometers). Its circumference is almost 25,000 miles (40,000 kilometers).

As far as we know, the earth is the only planet on which there is life. It is also the only one that has any water. If you look at the map of the world on page 4, you will see that the surface of the earth is made up of water and land areas. A little more than 70 percent of the world is water. The remaining part is land.

The great mass of water that covers most of the earth is often called the *world ocean*. It is made up of four major oceans: the Pacific Ocean, which is by far the largest, the Atlantic Ocean, the Indian Ocean, and the Arctic Ocean. The oceans are further subdivided into smaller bodies of water, such as seas, gulfs, and bays.

The floor of the ocean is not smooth. Like land above water, it has high mountains, flat areas, hills, volcanoes, and deep trenches. The greatest known depth of the oceans is located in the Pacific near the island of Guam. Here, Challenger Deep drops more than 36,000 feet (11,000 meters) beneath the rest of the ocean floor.

The remaining bodies of water on earth are inland. The largest inland body of water is the salty Caspian Sea, which is located between Europe and Asia. Although it is called a sea, the Caspian is actually a lake because it has no outlet to the ocean. The largest fresh water lake is Lake Superior in North America. The three longest rivers are, in order of length, the Nile of Africa, the Amazon of South America, and the Mississippi-Missouri of North America.

The oceans and other bodies of water play a very important part in our lives. People cannot live without water. Plants need it to grow. Water areas give us food and other natural resources. They are a source of electric power. They are used for transportation.

The land above water forms seven great landmasses called *continents*. Some scientists believe that about 250 million years ago there was only one giant landmass. This mass, which has been named *Pangaea*, gradually began to break apart. The sections slowly drifted in different directions. Forces within the land and the impact of the ocean water caused the continents to change shape. After millions of years, the landmasses became the seven continents of today. They are, in order of size: Asia, Africa, North America, South America, Antarctica, Europe, and Australia. Europe and Asia are often referred to together as "Eurasia."

In addition to the continents, there are thousands of smaller pieces of land above water. These islands often are near continents. In one place in the Pacific, thousands of islands stretch across the ocean. They are grouped under the name *Oceania*.

The continents differ from each other. Yet they all have the four major kinds of land: smooth lowlands, or plains; raised flatlands, or plateaus; hilly lands; and mountains. Look at the altitude scale on the map. All the areas under 1,600 feet (488 meters) are lowlands. In general, mountains are higher than hills, and they are more rugged and have many individual tall peaks. Different kinds of plants and animals are found at different heights in the mountains. The steep drops, cold temperatures, and high winds in many mountain areas make it difficult to build highways and railways in these regions.

The continents of Africa and Antarctica are mainly plateaus. The other continents have extensive plains or lowlands bordered in part by mountains or hills.

The mountains of the world can be grouped into two great mountain belts. One belt nearly encircles the Pacific Ocean. Starting in Antarctica, these mountains run northward along the west coast of South America and upwards through North America. The mountains then curve through the Aleutian Islands of Alaska and arc southward through the islands off the eastern coast of Asia to end in eastern Australia.

The second major belt centers in the Pamir mountainous region of Asia, just north of Pakistan where Afghanistan, India, Tajikistan, and China meet. From this central "knot," mountain ranges spread across Asia and Europe in three main arms. One extends north and northeast into China, Kazakhstan and Russia. The second group spreads east and southeast to separate China from India. It includes the Himalayas, where Mt. Everest, the highest mountain peak on earth, is located on the border of China and Nepal. This second group blocks the moisture-laden winds from the ocean, to help make the area to the north the "dry heart of Asia." The third branch extends west to Turkey, the Caucasus, and Europe. The Alps are part of this third group.

Throughout history, high mountains have hindered the spread of people and ideas. Nearly all of the world's large cities and densely populated areas are found in the plains, hilly lands, lower slopes of mountains, and in the broad river valleys of the uplands.

1. Explain what is meant by the term "continental drift."
2. List seven countries that occupy land north of the Arctic Circle.

NORTH AMERICA

North America is the third largest continent in size, after Asia and Africa. Situated in the northern half of the Western Hemisphere, the continent extends southwards over 5,000 miles (8,000 kilometers). It joins the continent of South America at the very narrow Isthmus of Panama. The section between Mexico and South America is called Central America, and it is often considered to be a subcontinent of North America.

The coastline of North America is very uneven. Great gulfs and bays reach into the mainland. The largest are Hudson Bay in the north, and the Gulf of Mexico and the Gulf of California in the south.

North America's larger islands are in the Arctic Ocean and in the Caribbean Sea. The largest island in the world, Greenland, is in the Arctic and most of it is covered with snow the year round.

Because it extends from the Arctic almost to the equator, North America has striking contrasts in climate. The temperature is always cold in the far north and always hot in the far south. The north is too cold for agriculture and very few people live there. In the Caribbean, the heat is cooled somewhat by ocean breezes. Unfortunately, most of the islands are in the path of hurricane winds, which destroy property and crops every year. The greater part of North America enjoys a temperate climate with warm summers and cold winters. Rainfall varies. There is over 80 inches of rainfall a year along the northwest Pacific coast and in the tropical rainforest areas of Central America and the Caribbean. There are dry areas also. The driest are in the deserts of the southwestern United States and of Mexico. In Death Valley, California, which is the lowest point in North America, there is less than two inches of rain a year.

Look at the map and compare the location of the United States with that of other countries in North America. Not only is it between Asia and Europe, it is also near South America. Its location is favorable for trade in all directions. Goods can be carried easily over inland waterway systems. The Great Lakes between Canada and the United States form the largest connected area of fresh water on earth. (Incidentally, North America has more lakes than any other continent.) The Great Lakes can be reached through the St. Lawrence Seaway—a series of canals, dams, and locks in the St. Lawrence River. South of the Great Lakes is the Mississippi-Missouri river system, which drains the central plains. Along with the Ohio River and about 250 other tributaries, it forms one of the greatest inland waterway systems in the world.

The principal geographical features of North America are its two mountain systems and the great central plains that lie between them. On the west coast, high and rugged mountains extend the entire length of the continent. In the north they begin at the tip of Alaska. The highest peak in North America, Mt. McKinley, is in Alaska. The western mountains include the Coast Ranges that hug the Pacific coast and the Rocky Mountains farther inland. The Rockies extend southward into Mexico, where they are called the Sierra Madre Oriental and the Sierra Madre Occidental. Lying between the Rocky Mountains and the coast ranges are lower areas—basins and plateaus. (A basin is an area that is lower than the surrounding land. It is shaped somewhat like a basin, or bowl.) The largest are the Columbia Plateau, the Colorado Plateau, and the Great Basin. These intermountain areas are dry and have harsh climates, but they are rich in minerals, and their scenery is spectacularly beautiful.

The other mountain system, the Appalachian Mountains, is in the east. This area is a mixture of mountain and plateau and extends from the Gulf of St. Lawrence almost to the Gulf of Mexico. The Appalachians are not very rugged. Their peaks are worn down and rounded. On the east they merge with the Piedmont Plateau, which slopes into the Atlantic Coastal Plain. The Appalachian region is rich in minerals and has many fertile river valleys. The rivers provide abundant water power for the area.

Surrounding Hudson Bay and covering about one-half of Canada is the Laurentian Plateau, or the Canadian Shield. It is a region of rock and poor soil and consists mainly of low-lying hills, rounded mountains, and many lakes. There is little agricultural land here, but the plateau is rich in minerals.

In the middle of North America, between the Rocky Mountains and the Appalachians are the central plains. The plains are shaped like a giant "V" and extend from southern Canada to the Gulf of Mexico. The western part of the region is called the Great Plains. The plains of southern Canada and northern United States are among the most fertile in the world. Other extensive lowlands in North America are in the southeastern United States and on the southeast coast of Mexico. The lowlands in the north are *tundra*—areas where the soil is frozen most of the year and where only a few low plants will grow.

---

1. List the seven countries of Central America.
2. What is the St. Lawrence Seaway? Why is it an important waterway?
3. What is the Canadian Shield?

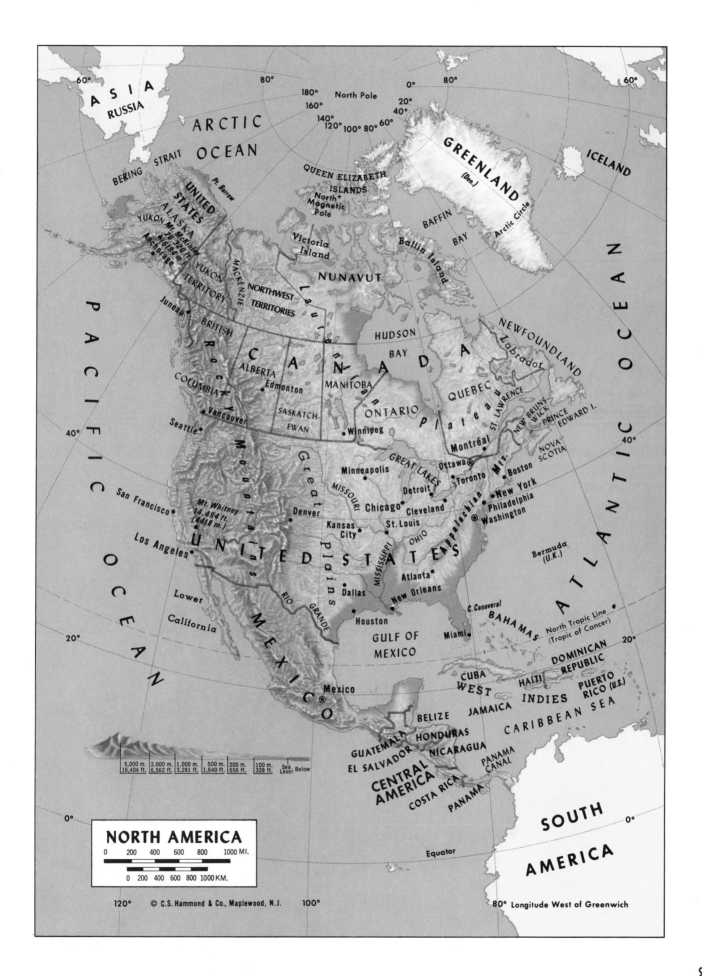

ASIA
RUSSIA

ARCTIC
OCEAN

BERING STRAIT

GREENLAND
(Den.)

ICELAND

UNITED
STATES
ALASKA
YUKON
Mt. McKinley
20,320 ft.
(6194 m.)
Anchorage
Juneau

Pt. Barrow

QUEEN ELIZABETH
ISLANDS
North+
Magnetic
Pole

Victoria
Island

BAFFIN
BAY

Arctic Circle

Baffin Island

YUKON
TERRITORY
BRITISH
COLUMBIA
ALBERTA
Edmonton
SASKATCH-
EWAN
Vancouver
Seattle

MACKENZIE

NORTHWEST
TERRITORIES

NUNAVUT

HUDSON
BAY

NEWFOUNDLAND
Labrador

C A N A D A

Laurentian

MANITOBA

ONTARIO

Winnipeg

QUEBEC

ST. LAWRENCE
NEW BRUNS-
WICK
PRINCE
EDWARD I.
Plateau
Montréal
NOVA
SCOTIA

PACIFIC

San Francisco
Los Angeles
Lower
California

Rocky
Mountains

Great Plains

Minneapolis
Denver
Kansas
City

MISSOURI

GREAT LAKES
Ottawa
Toronto
Detroit
Chicago
Cleveland
St. Louis
OHIO

Boston
New York
Philadelphia
Washington

Appalachian Mts.

Mt. Whitney
14,494 ft.
(4418 m.)

UNITED STATES

Bermuda
(U.K.)

O C E A N

MEXICO

RIO GRANDE

MISSISSIPPI

Dallas

Atlanta
New Orleans

Houston

C. Canaveral

Miami

GULF OF
MEXICO

BAHAMAS

North Tropic Line
(Tropic of Cancer)

ATLANTIC OCEAN

Mexico

CUBA
WEST
HAITI
INDIES
DOMINICAN
REPUBLIC
PUERTO
RICO (U.S.)

JAMAICA

CARIBBEAN SEA

BELIZE
GUATEMALA
HONDURAS
EL SALVADOR
NICARAGUA
PANAMA
CANAL
CENTRAL
AMERICA
COSTA RICA
PANAMA

SOUTH

AMERICA

Equator

5,000 m.   2,000 m.   1,000 m.   500 m.   200 m.   100 m.   Sea
16,404 ft. 6,562 ft. 3,281 ft. 1,640 ft. 656 ft. 328 ft. Level Below

NORTH AMERICA

0   200   400   600   800   1000 MI.

0   200   400   600   800 1000 KM.

© C.S. Hammond & Co., Maplewood, N.J.

80° Longitude West of Greenwich

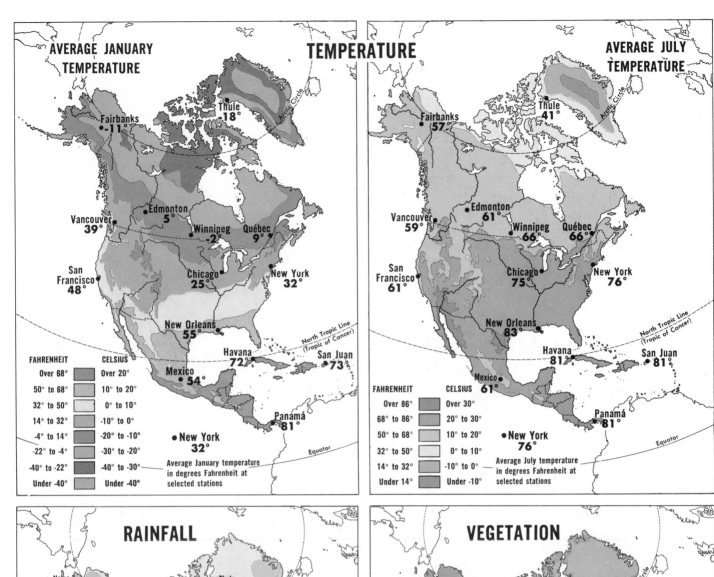

TEMPERATURE

AVERAGE JANUARY TEMPERATURE

Fairbanks -11°
Thule -18°
Edmonton 5°
Vancouver 39°
Winnipeg -2°
Québec 9°
San Francisco 48°
Chicago 25°
New York 32°
New Orleans 55°
Havana 72°
San Juan 73°
Mexico 54°
Panamá 81°

FAHRENHEIT	CELSIUS
Over 68°	Over 20°
50° to 68°	10° to 20°
32° to 50°	0° to 10°
14° to 32°	-10° to 0°
-4° to 14°	-20° to -10°
-22° to -4°	-30° to -20°
-40° to -22°	-40° to -30°
Under -40°	Under -40°

● New York 32°

Average January temperature in degrees Fahrenheit at selected stations

AVERAGE JULY TEMPERATURE

Fairbanks 57°
Thule 41°
Edmonton 61°
Vancouver 59°
Winnipeg 66°
Québec 66°
San Francisco 61°
Chicago 75°
New York 76°
New Orleans 83°
Havana 81°
San Juan 81°
Mexico 61°
Panamá 81°

FAHRENHEIT	CELSIUS
Over 86°	Over 30°
68° to 86°	20° to 30°
50° to 68°	10° to 20°
32° to 50°	0° to 10°
14° to 32°	-10° to 0°
Under 14°	Under -10°

● New York 76°

Average July temperature in degrees Fahrenheit at selected stations

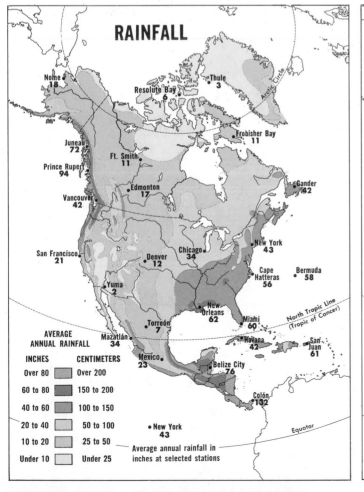

RAINFALL

Nome 18
Resolute Bay 6
Thule 3
Frobisher Bay 11
Juneau 72
Ft. Smith 11
Prince Rupert 94
Edmonton 17
Gander 42
Vancouver 42
San Francisco 21
Denver 12
Chicago 34
New York 43
Cape Hatteras 56
Bermuda 58
Yuma 2
New Orleans 62
Miami 60
Torreón 7
Mazatlán 34
Havana 42
San Juan 61
Mexico 23
Belize City 76
Colón 132

AVERAGE ANNUAL RAINFALL

INCHES	CENTIMETERS
Over 80	Over 200
60 to 80	150 to 200
40 to 60	100 to 150
20 to 40	50 to 100
10 to 20	25 to 50
Under 10	Under 25

● New York 43

Average annual rainfall in inches at selected stations

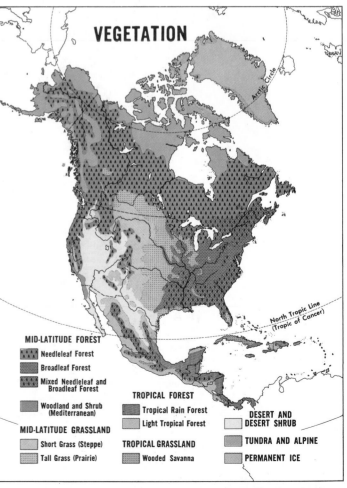

VEGETATION

MID-LATITUDE FOREST
Needleleaf Forest
Broadleaf Forest
Mixed Needleleaf and Broadleaf Forest
Woodland and Shrub (Mediterranean)

MID-LATITUDE GRASSLAND
Short Grass (Steppe)
Tall Grass (Prairie)

TROPICAL FOREST
Tropical Rain Forest
Light Tropical Forest

TROPICAL GRASSLAND
Wooded Savanna

DESERT AND DESERT SHRUB

TUNDRA AND ALPINE

PERMANENT ICE

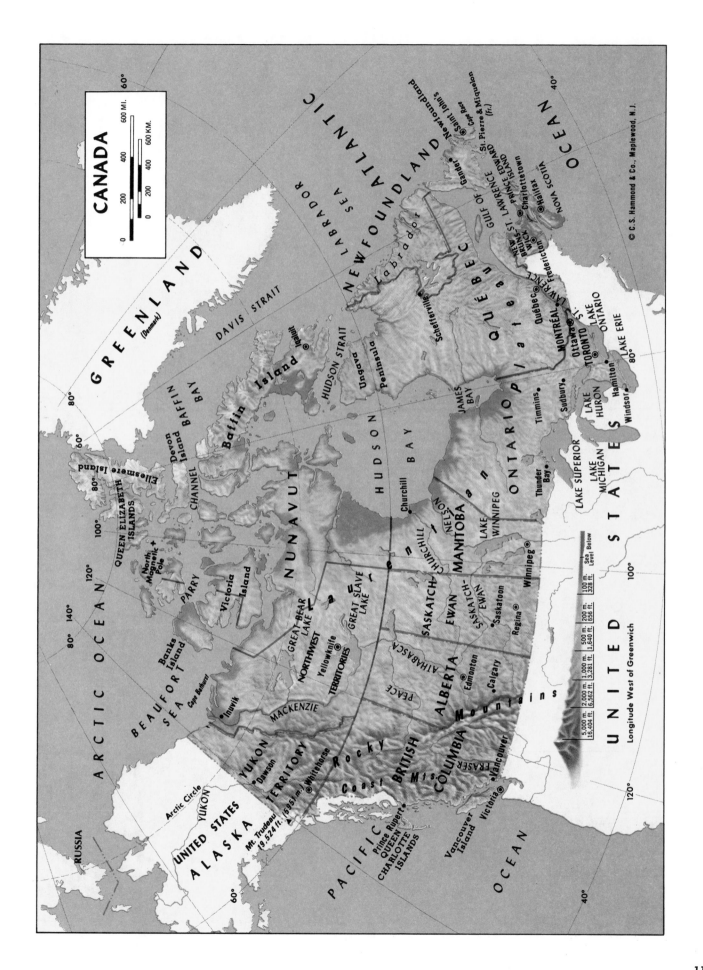

CANADA

600 MI.
400
600 KM.
200 400
0 200
0

© C.S. Hammond & Co., Maplewood, N.J.

RUSSIA

ARCTIC OCEAN

BEAUFORT SEA

Cape Bathurst

Inuvik

Banks Island

Victoria Island

PARRY CHANNEL

Queen Elizabeth Islands

North Magnetic Pole

Ellesmere Island

Devon Island

GREENLAND (Denmark)

DAVIS STRAIT

BAFFIN BAY

Baffin Island

Iqaluit

HUDSON STRAIT

Ungava

Ungava Peninsula

LABRADOR SEA

NEWFOUNDLAND

Labrador

ATLANTIC OCEAN

Newfoundland

Cape Race

Saint John's

St. Pierre & Miquelon (Fr.)

Gander

GULF OF ST. LAWRENCE

PRINCE EDWARD ISLAND

Charlottetown

NOVA SCOTIA

Halifax

NEW BRUNS-WICK

Fredericton

ST. LAWRENCE

QUÉBEC

Québec

MONTRÉAL

Ottawa

TORONTO

LAKE ONTARIO

LAKE ERIE

Hamilton

Windsor

ONTARIO Plateau

Timmins

Sudbury

Thunder Bay

LAKE SUPERIOR

LAKE MICHIGAN

LAKE HURON

JAMES BAY

HUDSON BAY

Churchill

CHURCHILL

NELSON

MANITOBA

LAKE WINNIPEG

Winnipeg

Schefferville

NUNAVUT

GREAT BEAR LAKE

GREAT SLAVE LAKE

Yellowknife

NORTHWEST TERRITORIES

MACKENZIE

SASKATCH- EWAN

Saskatoon

Regina

SASKATCH- EWAN

ATHABASCA

PEACE

ALBERTA

Edmonton

Calgary

Mountains

UNITED STATES

YUKON TERRITORY

YUKON

Dawson

Whitehorse

Arctic Circle

UNITED STATES

ALASKA

Mt. Trudeau 19,524 ft. (5,951 m.)

Rocky

Coast Mts.

BRITISH COLUMBIA

FRASER

Prince Rupert

QUEEN CHARLOTTE ISLANDS

Vancouver Island

Victoria

Vancouver

PACIFIC OCEAN

100° Longitude West of Greenwich

5,000 m. 16,404 ft. | 2,000 m. 6,562 ft. | 1,000 m. 3,281 ft. | 500 m. 1,640 ft. | 200 m. 656 ft. | 100 m. 328 ft. | Sea Level | Sea Below

60°
40°
80°
60°
80°
100°
120°
140°
120°
100°
40°

11

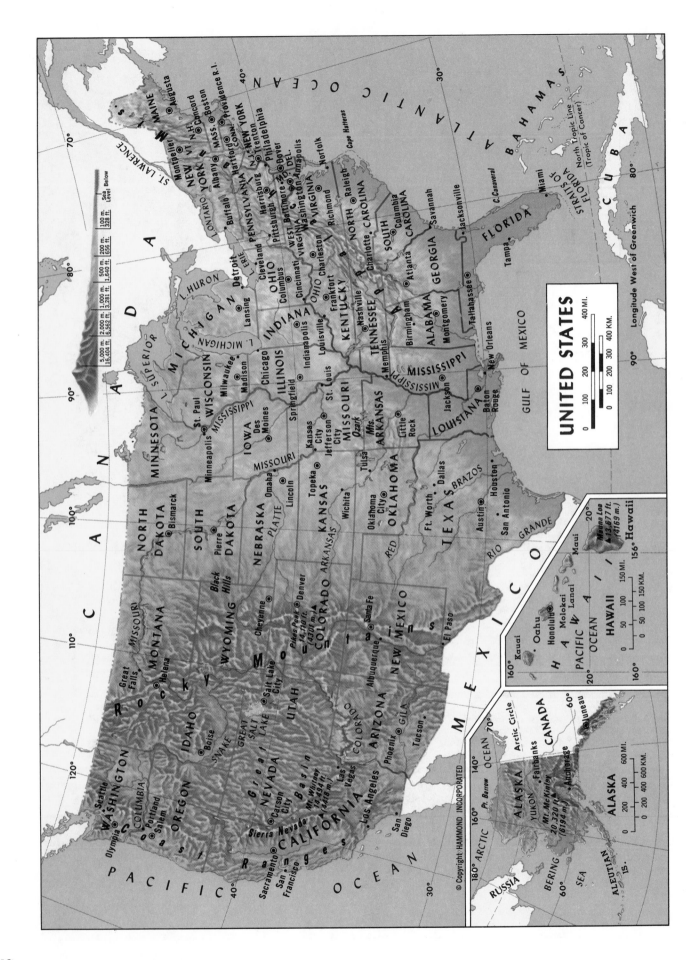

UNITED STATES

12

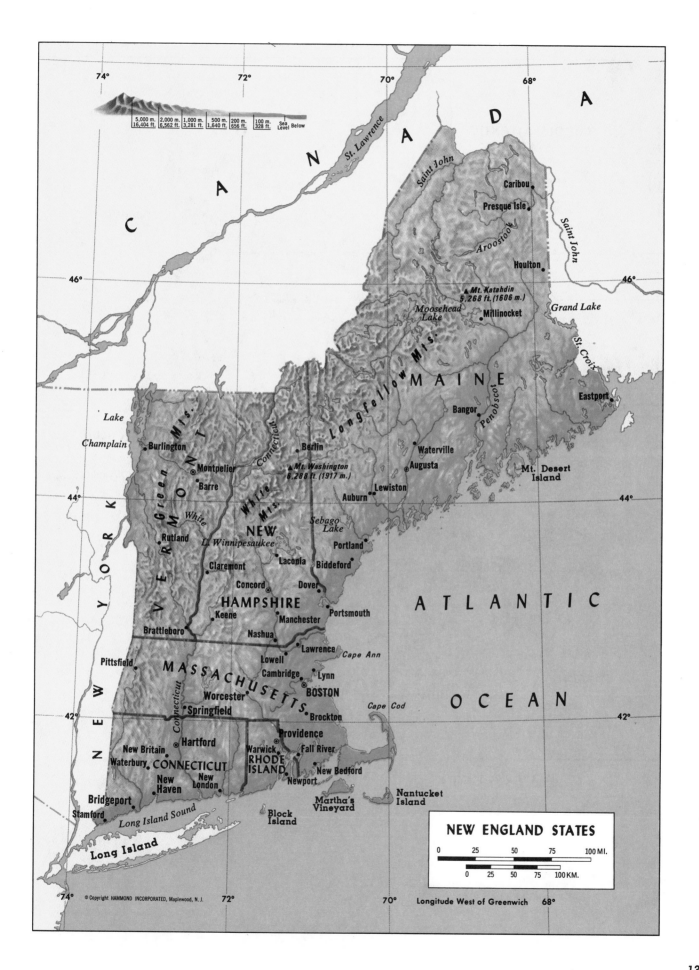

74° 72° 70° 68°

5,000 m. 2,000 m. 1,000 m. 500 m. 200 m. 100 m. Sea Below
16,404 ft. 6,562 ft. 3,281 ft. 1,640 ft. 656 ft. 328 ft. Level

C A N A D A

St. Lawrence

Saint John

Caribou

Presque Isle

Aroostook

Saint John

46° 46°
Houlton

▲ Mt. Katahdin
5,268 ft. (1606 m.)

Moosehead
Lake Millinocket Grand Lake

St. Croix

M A I N E

Longfellow Mts.

Penobscot

Eastport

Lake Bangor

Champlain Burlington Berlin Waterville

Montpelier Mt. Washington Augusta Mt. Desert
6,288 ft. (1917 m.) Island

VERMONT Green Mts. Connecticut Lewiston

Barre White Mts. Auburn

44° White Sebago 44°
Rutland NEW Lake

L. Winnipesaukee Portland

Claremont Laconia Biddeford

Concord Dover

HAMPSHIRE A T L A N T I C

Keene Manchester Portsmouth

Brattleboro Nashua

Pittsfield Lawrence Cape Ann

Lowell O C E A N
Cambridge Lynn

MASSACHUSETTS BOSTON

Connecticut Worcester

Springfield Brockton

42° Cape Cod 42°
Hartford Providence

New Britain Warwick Fall River

Waterbury CONNECTICUT RHODE New Bedford
ISLAND

New New Newport Nantucket
Haven London Island

Bridgeport Martha's
Vineyard

Stamford Long Island Sound Block
Island

Long Island

© Copyright HAMMOND INCORPORATED, Maplewood, N.J.

N E W   Y O R K

NEW ENGLAND STATES

0 25 50 75 100 MI.

0 25 50 75 100 KM.

74° 72° 70° Longitude West of Greenwich 68°

13

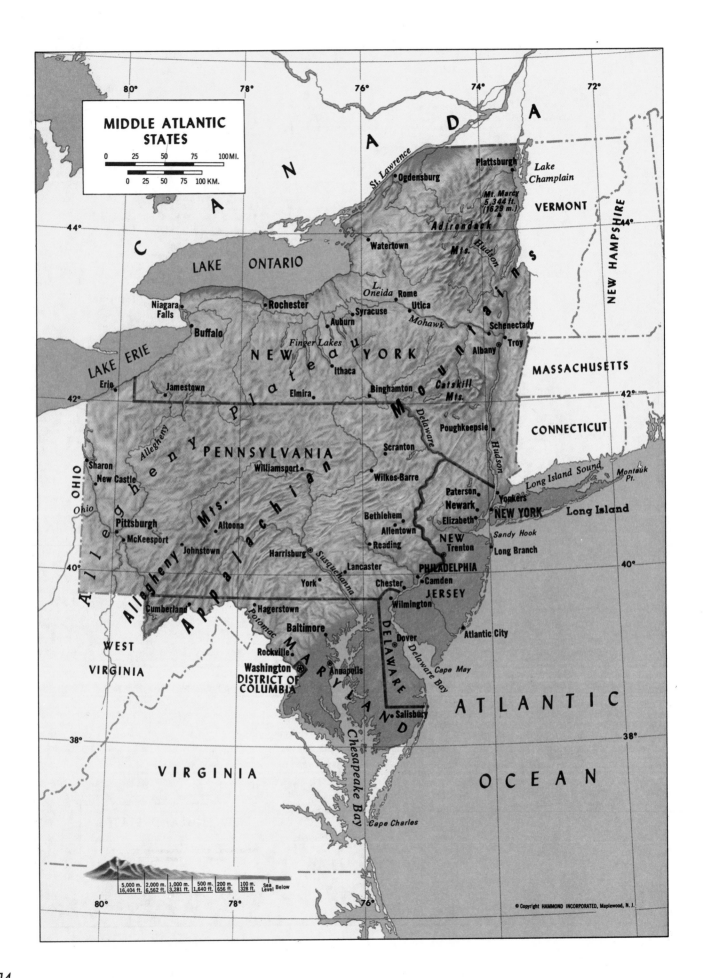

MIDDLE ATLANTIC STATES

0 25 50 75 100 MI.

0 25 50 75 100 KM.

C A N A D A

VERMONT

NEW HAMPSHIRE

St. Lawrence
Ogdensburg
Plattsburgh
Lake Champlain
Mt. Marcy 5,344 ft. (1629 m.)
Adirondack Mts.
Watertown
Hudson

LAKE ONTARIO

L. Oneida
Rome
Niagara Falls
Rochester
Syracuse
Utica
Schenectady
Auburn
Mohawk
Buffalo
Finger Lakes
Troy
Albany

NEW YORK

LAKE ERIE

MASSACHUSETTS

Ithaca
Elmira
Binghamton
Catskill Mts.

Erie
Jamestown
Allegheny Plateau

Poughkeepsie
CONNECTICUT

Delaware
Hudson

Allegheny
Scranton
Long Island Sound
Montauk Pt.

PENNSYLVANIA

Sharon
New Castle
Williamsport
Wilkes-Barre
Paterson
Yonkers
NEW YORK
Long Island

OHIO

Ohio
Allegheny Mts.
Altoona
Bethlehem
Newark
Elizabeth
Sandy Hook

Pittsburgh
Appalachian
Allentown
NEW
Trenton
Long Branch

McKeesport
Johnstown
Harrisburg
Reading
JERSEY

Lancaster
PHILADELPHIA
Camden

York
Susquehanna
Chester
Wilmington

Cumberland
Hagerstown
DELAWARE
Atlantic City

WEST
VIRGINIA

Potomac
Baltimore
Rockville
Dover
Delaware Bay

MARYLAND

Washington
DISTRICT OF COLUMBIA
Annapolis
Cape May

Salisbury

ATLANTIC

VIRGINIA

Chesapeake Bay
Cape Charles

OCEAN

5,000 m. 16,404 ft. 2,000 m. 6,562 ft. 1,000 m. 3,281 ft. 500 m. 1,640 ft. 200 m. 656 ft. 100 m. 328 ft. Sea Level Below

© Copyright HAMMOND INCORPORATED, Maplewood, N.J.

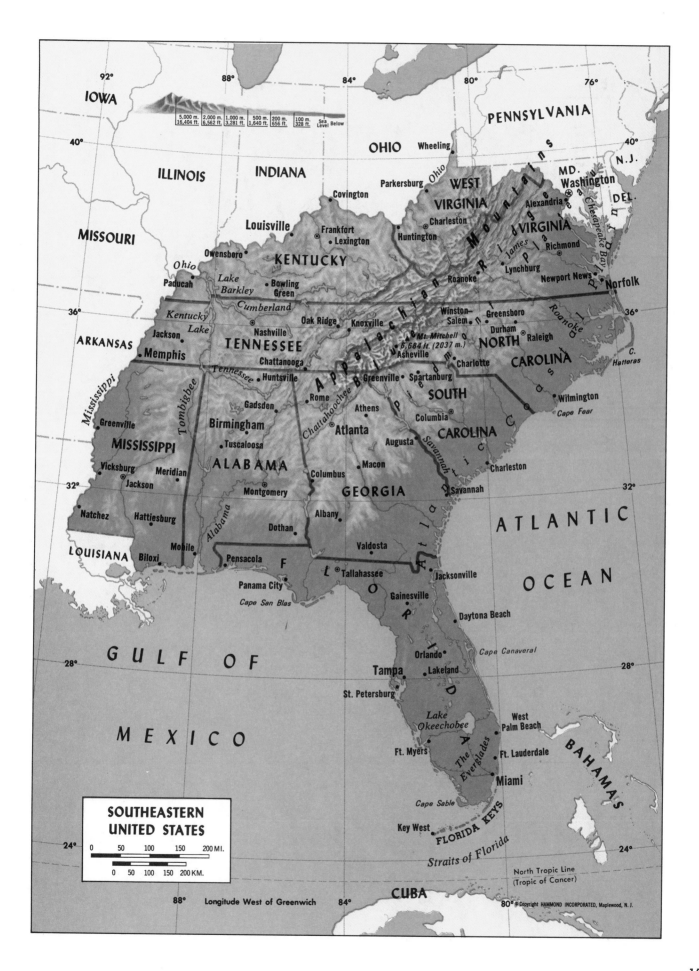

SOUTHEASTERN
UNITED STATES

0   50   100   150   200 MI.

0   50   100   150   200 KM.

5,000 m. 2,000 m. 1,000 m. 500 m. 200 m. 100 m. Sea
16,404 ft. 6,562 ft. 3,281 ft. 1,640 ft. 656 ft. 328 ft. Level Below

Longitude West of Greenwich

North Tropic Line
(Tropic of Cancer)

© Copyright HAMMOND INCORPORATED, Maplewood, N.J.

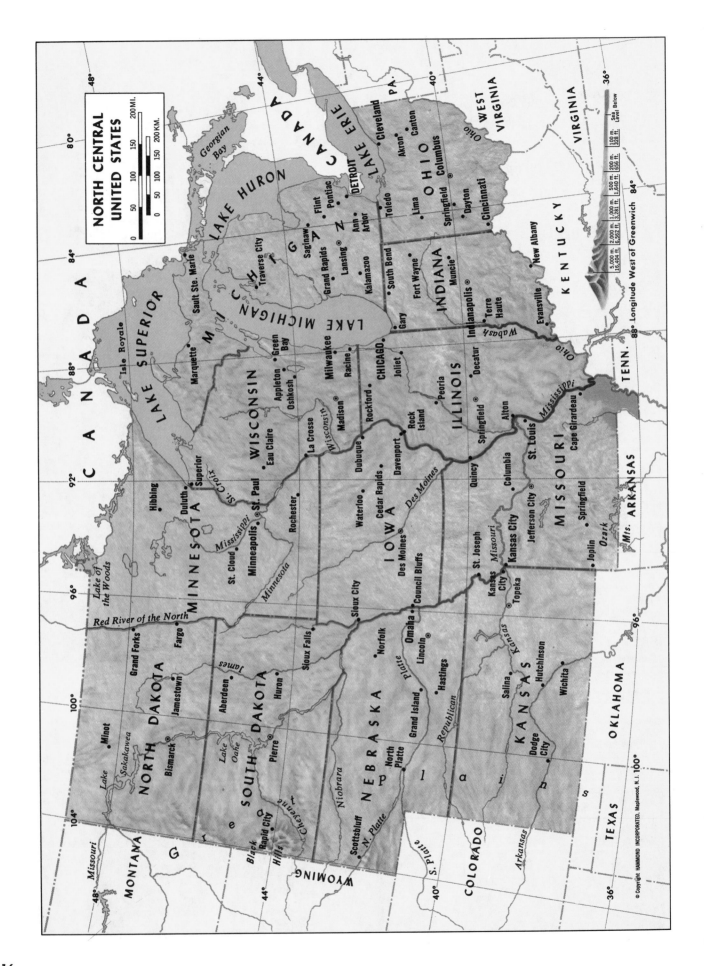

NORTH CENTRAL
UNITED STATES

200 MI.
150
100
50
0

200 KM.
150
100
50
0

5,000 m. 2,000 m. 1,000 m. 500 m. 200 m. 100 m. Sea Below
16,404 ft. 6,562 ft. 3,281 ft. 1,640 ft. 656 ft. 328 ft. Level

16

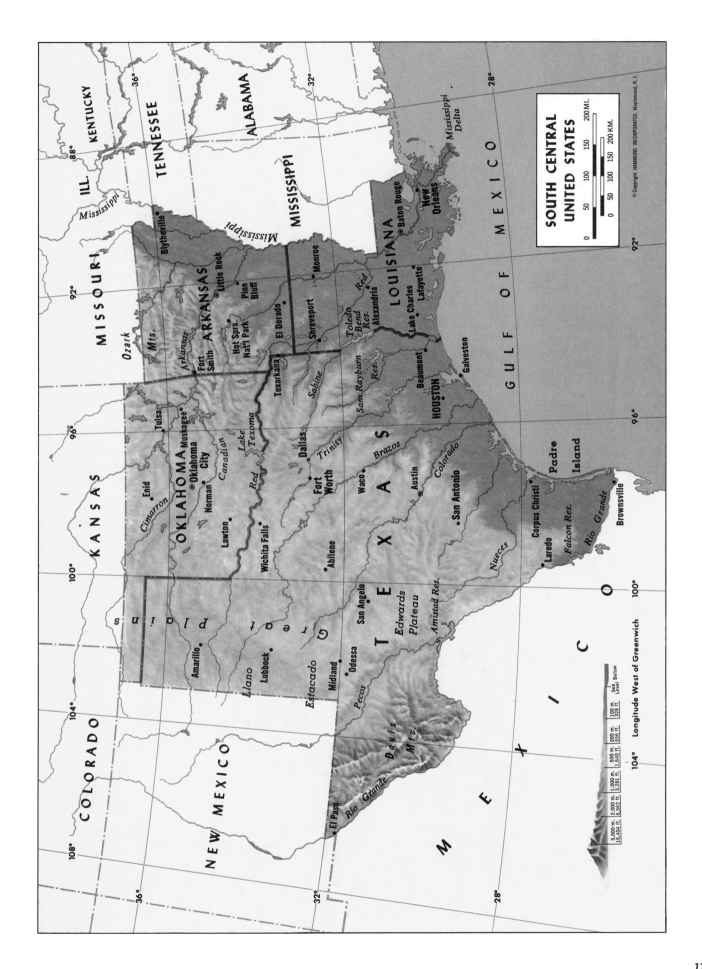

KENTUCKY
ILL.
TENNESSEE
ALABAMA
MISSISSIPPI

Mississippi

Mississippi
Blytheville

MISSOURI

Ozark
Mts.

ARKANSAS
Little Rock
Pine Bluff
Monroe

Arkansas
Fort Smith
Hot Sprs. Nat'l Park
El Dorado
Shreveport

LOUISIANA
Baton Rouge
New Orleans
Mississippi Delta

GULF OF MEXICO

Red
Toledo Bend Res.
Alexandria
Lake Charles
Lafayette

KANSAS

Tulsa
Muskogee

OKLAHOMA
Oklahoma City
Norman
Enid

Cimarron

Canadian
Lake Texoma
Red

Dallas
Trinity
Sabine
Sam Rayburn Res.
Beaumont
Galveston

HOUSTON

Lawton
Wichita Falls

Fort Worth
Waco
Brazos
Austin

Colorado

T E X A S

San Antonio

Padre Island

Corpus Christi

Abilene

Nueces
Laredo
Falcon Res.
Rio Grande
Brownsville

San Angelo
Edwards Plateau
Amistad Res.

Great Plains

Amarillo
Lubbock
Midland
Odessa
Estacado
Llano

Pecos

Davis Mts.

Rio Grande
El Paso

NEW MEXICO

COLORADO

M E X I C O

SOUTH CENTRAL
UNITED STATES

200 MI.
0   50   100   150
0   50   100   150   200 KM.

© Copyright HAMMOND INCORPORATED, Maplewood, N.J.

Longitude West of Greenwich

5,000 m.   2,000 m.   1,000 m.   500 m.   200 m.   100 m.   Sea
16,404 ft. 6,562 ft. 3,281 ft. 1,640 ft. 656 ft. 328 ft. Level Below

108° 104° 100° 96° 92° 88°
36° 32° 28°

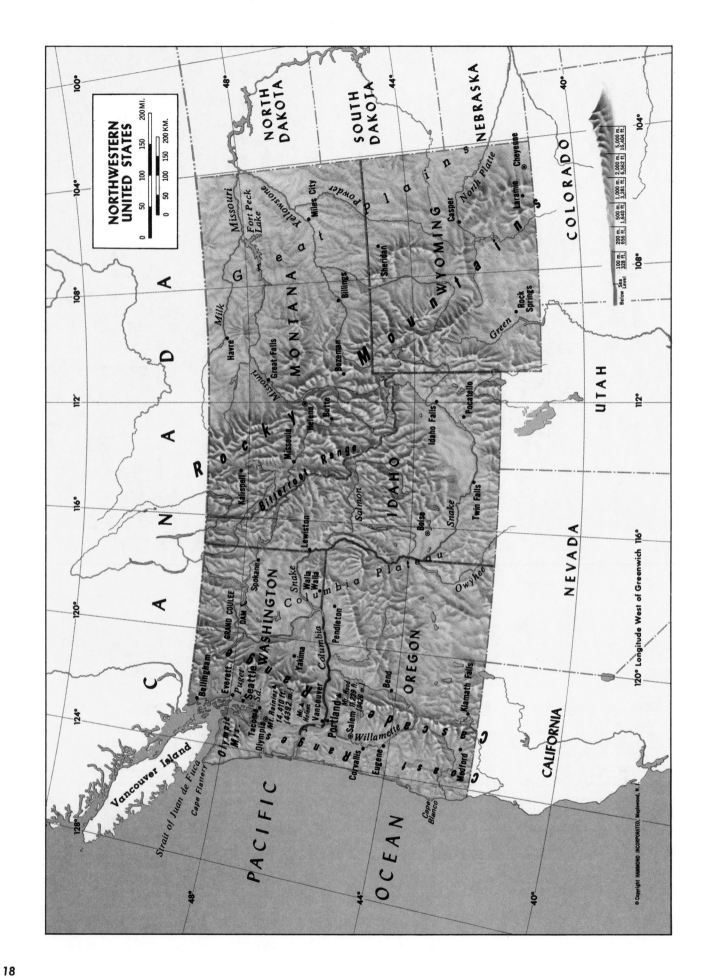

NORTHWESTERN
UNITED STATES

© Copyright HAMMOND INCORPORATED, Maplewood, N.J.

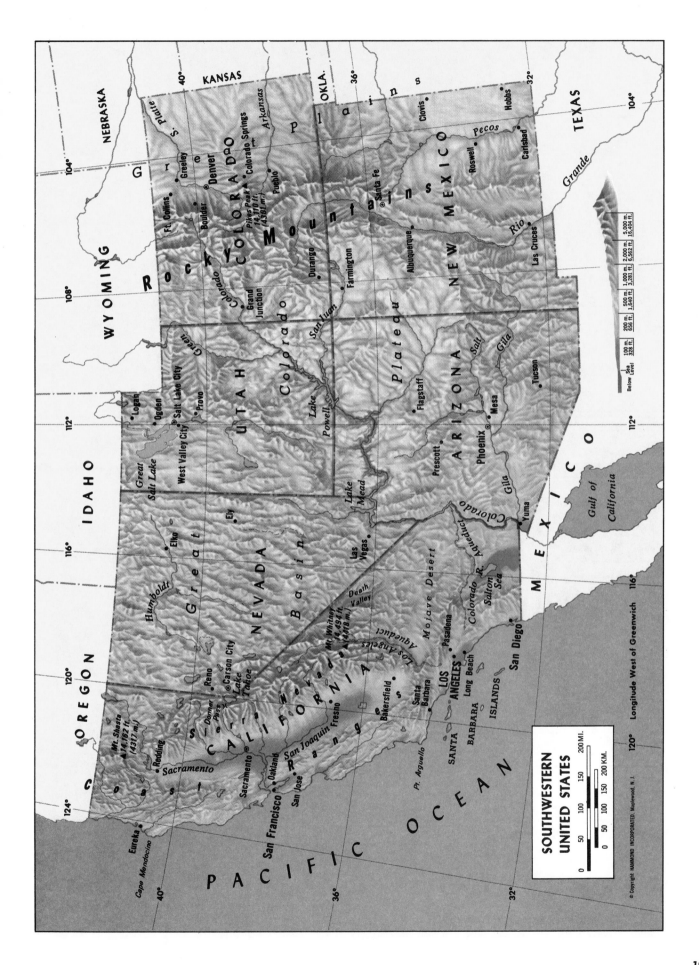

NEBRASKA

KANSAS

OKLA.

TEXAS

WYOMING

COLORADO

Rocky Mountains

Great Plains

S. Platte

Greeley

Ft. Collins

Boulder

⊚Denver

Colorado Springs

Pikes Peak 14,110 ft. (4301 m.)

Pueblo

Arkansas

Santa Fe ⊚

Clovis

Hobbs

Pecos

Roswell

Carlsbad

NEW MEXICO

Durango

Farmington

Albuquerque

Rio

Grande

Las Cruces

Grand Junction

Colorado

San Juan

Plateau

Salt

Gila

IDAHO

Green

UTAH

Colorado

Lake Powell

ARIZONA

Rio

Logan

Ogden

Salt Lake City

Provo

West Valley City

Great Salt Lake

Flagstaff

Prescott

Phoenix ⊚

Mesa

Tucson

Lake Mead

Gila

MEXICO

Gulf of California

OREGON

Elko

Ely

NEVADA

Great Basin

Humboldt

Las Vegas

Death Valley

Mojave Desert

Colorado R.

Yuma

Colorado Aqueduct

Salton Sea

5,000 m. 16,404 ft.
2,000 m. 6,562 ft.
1,000 m. 3,281 ft.
500 m. 1,640 ft.
200 m. 656 ft.
100 m. 328 ft.
Sea Level
Below Sea Level

Reno

Carson City

Lake Tahoe

Donner Pass

Mt. Whitney 14,494 ft. (4418 m.)

Sierra Nevada

Los Angeles Aqueduct

Pasadena

San Diego

CALIFORNIA

Mt. Shasta 14,162 ft. (4317 m.)

Redding

Sacramento

Sacramento

Oakland

San Jose

San Francisco

San Joaquin

Fresno

Bakersfield

Santa Barbara

Pt. Arguello

LOS ANGELES

Long Beach

SANTA BARBARA ISLANDS

Coast

Ranges

Eureka

Cape Mendocino

PACIFIC OCEAN

SOUTHWESTERN UNITED STATES

© Copyright HAMMOND INCORPORATED, Maplewood, N.J.

0   50   100   150   200 MI.
0   50   100   150   200 KM.

Longitude West of Greenwich

40°

104°

104°

108°

112°

116°

120°

124°

40°

36°

36°

32°

112°

116°

120°

ALASKA

0 100 200 300 400 500 MI.

0 100 200 300 400 500 KM.

ARCTIC OCEAN

Barrow • Pt. Barrow
• Prudhoe Bay

CHUKCHI
SEA

Pt. Hope

Colville
Brooks Range

Arctic Circle

CANADA

ASIA

RUSSIA

Bering Strait

Seward
Peninsula

Koyukuk

Yukon

Nome • Norton
Sound

Fairbanks

Tanana

St. Lawrence I.

60°

60°

St. Mathew
I.

Bethel •

Yukon

Kuskokwim

Alaska Range

▲ Mt. McKinley
20,320 ft.
(6194 m.)

Wrangell Mts.

St. Elias Mts.

Anchorage •

• Kenai
Kenai
Pen.

Cordova •

Coast Mts.

BERING

Nunivak
I.

Cook Inlet

Juneau •

SEA

Kuskokwim
Bay

Range

Aleutian

Gulf of Alaska

ALEXANDER

Sitka •

PRIBILOF
ISLANDS

Bristol Bay

Alaska Peninsula

Kodiak •

Kodiak I.

ARCHIPELAGO

Ketchikan •

Attu I.

Unimak
I.

Unalaska
I.

Unmak I.

PACIFIC OCEAN

Kiska I.

Atka I.

ALEUTIAN ISLANDS

50°

50°

Below Sea
Level 100 m.
328 ft. 200 m.
656 ft. 500 m.
1,640 ft. 1,000 m.
3,281 ft. 2,000 m.
6,562 ft. 5,000 m.
16,404 ft.

© Copyright HAMMOND INCORPORATED, Maplewood, N.J.

Longitude West 140° of Greenwich

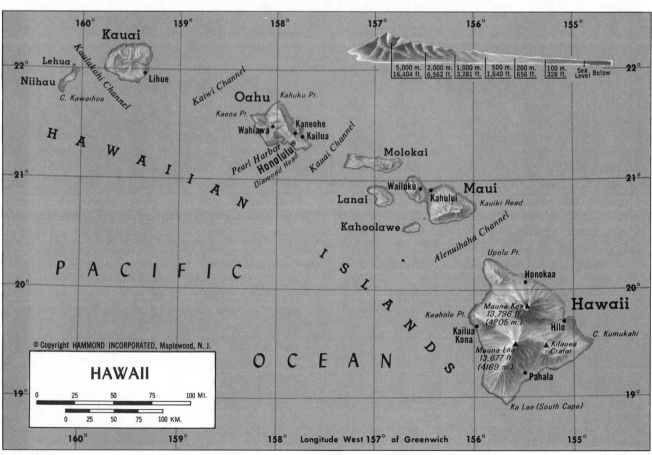

Kauai

Lehua
Niihau
Kaulakahi Channel
C. Kawaihoa

Lihue •

22°

22°

5,000 m.
16,404 ft. 2,000 m.
6,562 ft. 1,000 m.
3,281 ft. 500 m.
1,640 ft. 200 m.
656 ft. 100 m.
328 ft. Sea
Level Below

Kaiwi Channel

Oahu

Kahuku Pt.

Kaena Pt.

Wahiawa •

Kaneohe •
• Kailua

Pearl Harbor

Honolulu

Diamond Head

Kauai Channel

Molokai

21°

21°

HAWAIIAN

Lanai

Wailuku •
Kahului •

Maui

Kauiki Head

Kahoolawe

Alenuihaha Channel

Upolu Pt.

PACIFIC

Honokaa •

20°

20°

Keahole Pt.

Mauna Kea
13,796 ft.
(4205 m.) ▲

Hawaii

Kailua
Kona •

Hilo •

C. Kumukahi

© Copyright HAMMOND INCORPORATED, Maplewood, N.J.

ISLANDS

Mauna Loa
13,677 ft.
(4169 m.) ▲

▲ Kilauea
Crater

HAWAII

0 25 50 75 100 MI.

0 25 50 75 100 KM.

19°

OCEANS

Pahala •

19°

Ka Lae (South Cape)

Longitude West 157° of Greenwich

20

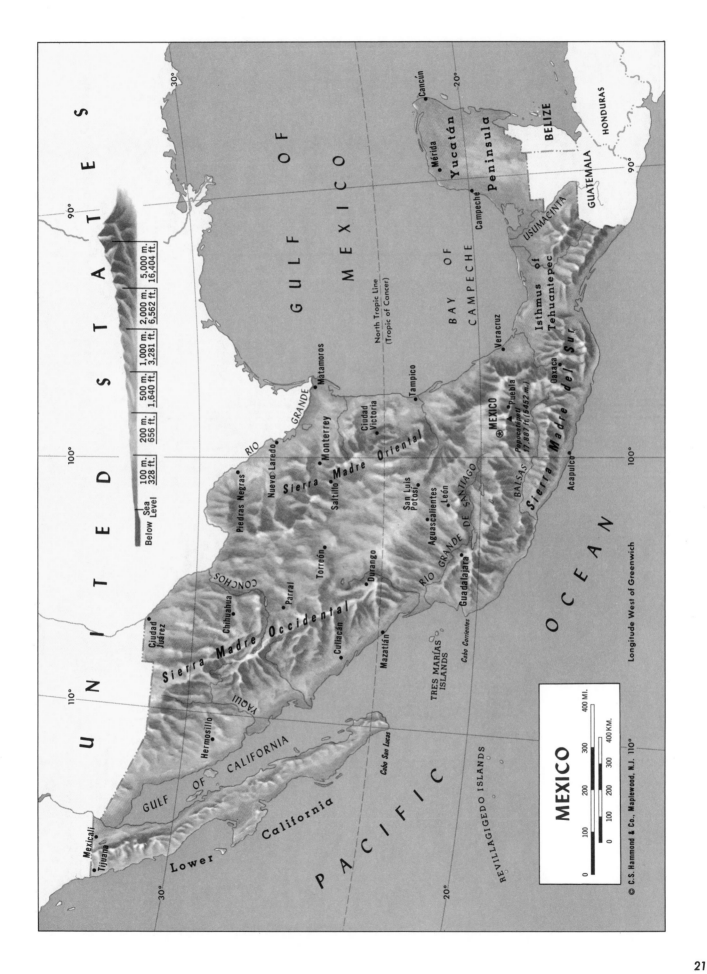

MEXICO

UNITED STATES

GULF OF MEXICO

PACIFIC OCEAN

Below Sea Level | 100 m. 328 ft. | 200 m. 656 ft. | 500 m. 1,640 ft. | 1,000 m. 3,281 ft. | 2,000 m. 6,562 ft. | 5,000 m. 16,404 ft.

Cancún
Mérida
Yucatán Peninsula
Campeche
BELIZE
HONDURAS
GUATEMALA
USUMACINTA
Isthmus of Tehuantepec
BAY OF CAMPECHE
North Tropic Line (Tropic of Cancer)
Veracruz
Oaxaca
Sierra Madre del Sur
Tampico
Puebla
MEXICO
Popocatépetl 17,887 ft. (5452 m.)
Ciudad Victoria
Sierra Madre Oriental
Acapulco
Matamoros
RIO GRANDE
Nuevo Laredo
Monterrey
Saltillo
San Luis Potosí
León
Aguascalientes
GRANDE DE SANTIAGO
BALSAS
Piedras Negras
RIO GRANDE
Guadalajara
CONCHOS
Torreón
Durango
Parral
Chihuahua
Ciudad Juárez
Sierra Madre Occidental
Culiacán
Mazatlán
YAQUI
Hermosillo
GULF OF CALIFORNIA
Cabo San Lucas
Cabo Corrientes
TRES MARÍAS ISLANDS
Lower California
Mexicali
Tijuana
REVILLAGIGEDO ISLANDS

Longitude West of Greenwich

MEXICO

0   100   200   300   400 MI.
0   100   200   300   400 KM.

© C.S. Hammond & Co., Maplewood, N.J. 110°

21

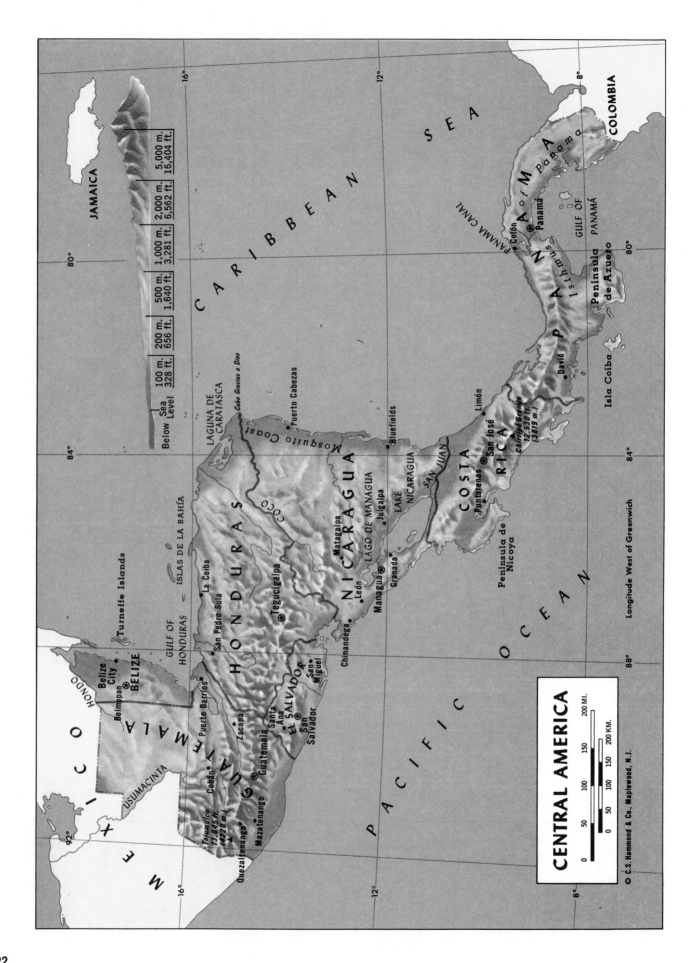

CENTRAL AMERICA

JAMAICA

Below Sea Level · 100 m. 328 ft. · 200 m. 656 ft. · 500 m. 1,640 ft. · 1,000 m. 3,281 ft. · 2,000 m. 6,562 ft. · 5,000 m. 16,404 ft.

C A R I B B E A N   S E A

COLOMBIA

GULF OF PANAMÁ

PANAMA

Panamá
Colón
PANAMA CANAL
Isthmus of Panama
David
Isla Coiba

Peninsula de Azuero

COSTA RICA
San José
Limón
Puntarenas
Chirripó Grande 12,530 ft. (3819 m.)
Peninsula de Nicoya

SAN JUAN
LAKE NICARAGUA
LAGO DE MANAGUA

NICARAGUA
Bluefields
Puerto Cabezas
Cabo Gracias a Dios
LAGUNA DE CARATASCA
Mosquito Coast
Coco
Matagalpa
Juigalpa
Managua
Granada
León
Chinandega

HONDURAS
La Ceiba
San Pedro Sula
Tegucigalpa
GULF OF HONDURAS
ISLAS DE LA BAHÍA
Turneffe Islands

EL SALVADOR
San Miguel
San Salvador
Santa Ana
San

GUATEMALA
Guatemala
Cobán
Zacapa
Mazatenango
Quezaltenango
Tajumulco 13,845 ft. (4220 m.)
Puerto Barrios
USUMACINTA

BELIZE
Belize City
Belmopan
HONDO

MEXICO

P A C I F I C   O C E A N

Longitude West of Greenwich

CENTRAL AMERICA

0 50 100 150 200 MI.
0 50 100 150 200 KM.

© C.S. Hammond & Co., Maplewood, N.J.

22

CENTRAL AMERICA

Connecting the North American and South American continents is a long, narrow stretch of land called an isthmus. This area is often called Central America even though it is the southernmost part of North America. The seven independent nations that form Central America are bounded on the west by the Pacific Ocean and on the east by the Caribbean Sea.

Because almost all of Central America lies between the equator and 18° north latitude, the climate is relatively hot, and rainfall frequent. The highest point in Central America, Tajumulco, Guatemala, is 13,845 feet above sea level. Many of the mountains that form Central America are active volcanos.

The sunshine and rainfall, combined with the fertile Central American soil, support thriving farming and livestock industries. Coffee, sugarcane, bananas, cotton, rice and livestock, the chief Central American agricultural products, are the major exports.

Since prehistoric times, the isthmus has served as a passageway for animals, and later people migrating first to South America and, then, back and forth between the continents.

Native American Indians were among the early inhabitants of Central America. In the 1500s, however, the Spanish conquered the Indians. Today, the population of Central America is a mixture of people of Indian, European, Asian, and African descent.

In 1903, the United States and Panama established a treaty which gave the United States the right to build a canal through Panama. Find the Panama Canal on your map. The United States was given exclusive control of the canal, and in 1914 it was opened. However, for many years Panamanians wanted to amend the treaty and limit American control over the waterway. In 1977, under the Carter Administration, the United States and Panama signed a new treaty. This new treaty resulted in the transfer of the canal to Panama, which took place in the year 2000.

1. Look at the map of the world on page 4. Why does it make sense to build a canal through Central America? What would be the effect on worldwide shipping were the canal not there?
2. Find El Salvador on the map. The pressure of over-population has led to constant political unrest within this nation. In addition, the dense population has led its neighbors to fear that El Salvador might attempt to expand into their territories. Research the history of this country from 1969, and try to find other reasons for the political unrest. What role has the United States played in the recent history of this country? Why are Americans divided about the role of the United States in El Salvador? This information is readily available on the internet.

THE WEST INDIES MAP—PAGE 24

East of Central America and Mexico lie the West Indies. This group of islands has two major divisions: the Greater Antilles and the Lesser Antilles. The Greater Antilles, the larger group of islands, includes Cuba, Jamaica, Hispaniola (Haiti and the Dominican Republic share the island), and Puerto Rico. The islands of the Lesser Antilles extend southerly from Puerto Rico to Trinidad and west to Aruba.

The climate in the West Indies is warm all year around. Ample rainfall and cool breezes offset the very warm temperatures during June, July and August.

The West Indies are formed by mountains whose peaks reach above the sea. The highest point is Pico Duarte in the Dominican Republic (10,417 feet). Some of the islands in the Lesser Antilles are active volcanos.

Because most of the islands lack mineral resources, except for limited minerals in Trinidad, Cuba and Jamaica, the economy of the islands depends heavily on farming. Tropical fruits, coffee, sugar and spices are among the farm products. Sugar cane is the leading product.

Some of the islands have advanced economically through limited industrialization. Puerto Rico was one of the first islands to successfully develop industry.

Tourism has also stimulated the economy of the West Indies. Over the past 20 years, income from both tourism and industry has led to a higher standard of living on the islands. Some of the islands, however, are still poverty-ridden because of overpopulation. On several islands, civil strife and political instability have also hindered economic growth.

When Columbus discovered the West Indies, Indians occupied the islands. Then, as more Europeans began migrating to the islands, the Indian population declined. Europeans also brought slaves from Africa. Many descendants of these slaves have remained on the islands. Today, on most of the islands, the population is composed of many different ethnic groups.

1. The history of the Dominican Republic is plagued by violence and bloodshed. Research the history of this country. Then study the Dominican Republic today. How has the unrest in this country affected its growth? If you had to speculate on the future of the Dominican Republic, what conclusions would you draw, based upon its past? What improvements do you see? What problems do you see?

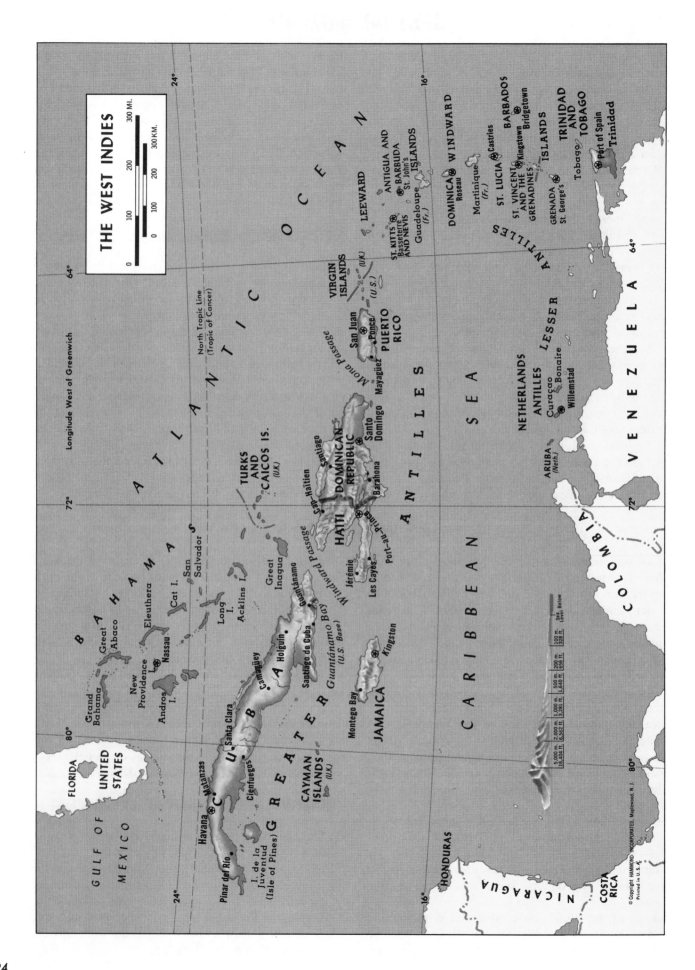

THE WEST INDIES

300 MI.

300 KM.

0   100   200

0   100   200

GULF OF MEXICO

FLORIDA
UNITED STATES

Grand Bahama
Great Abaco
New Providence I.
Nassau
Andros I.
Eleuthera
San Salvador
Cat I.
Long I.
Acklins I.
Great Inagua

B A H A M A S

Pinar del Río
Havana
Matanzas
I. de la Juventud (Isle of Pines)
Cienfuegos
Santa Clara
Camagüey
Holguín
Santiago de Cuba

C U B A

G R E A T E R

CAYMAN ISLANDS (U.K.)

Montego Bay
Kingston
JAMAICA

Guantánamo
Guantánamo Bay (U.S. Base)

Windward Passage

Cap-Haïtien
HAITI
Jérémie
Les Cayes
Port-au-Prince

TURKS AND CAICOS IS. (U.K.)

Santiago
Santo Domingo
DOMINICAN REPUBLIC
Barahona

Mona Passage

Mayagüez
San Juan
Ponce
PUERTO RICO

VIRGIN ISLANDS
(U.K.)
(U.S.)

A N T I L L E S

LEEWARD

ST. KITTS
Basseterre
AND NEVIS

ANTIGUA AND BARBUDA
St. John's

Guadeloupe (Fr.)
ISLANDS

DOMINICA
Roseau

Martinique (Fr.)

ST. LUCIA
Castries

ST. VINCENT
AND THE GRENADINES
Kingstown

BARBADOS
Bridgetown

WINDWARD

GRENADA
St. George's

ISLANDS

Tobago
Port of Spain
Trinidad
TRINIDAD AND TOBAGO

A N T I L L E S

L E S S E R

NETHERLANDS ANTILLES
Curaçao
Bonaire
Willemstad

ARUBA (Neth.)

C A R I B B E A N   S E A

HONDURAS
NICARAGUA
COSTA RICA

C O L O M B I A

V E N E Z U E L A

A T L A N T I C   O C E A N

North Tropic Line (Tropic of Cancer)

Longitude West of Greenwich

24°   80°   72°   64°   16°

5,000 m.
16,404 ft.   2,000 m.
6,562 ft.   1,000 m.
3,281 ft.   500 m.
1,640 ft.   200 m.
656 ft.   100 m.
328 ft.   Sea Level   Below

© Copyright HAMMOND INCORPORATED, Maplewood, N.J.
Printed in U.S.A.

24

SOUTH AMERICA

South America is the fourth largest continent and the southernmost of the two continents in the Western Hemisphere. It is connected to North America at the Isthmus of Panama. Most of South America lies south of the equator, and it extends southwards to about 600 miles (970 kilometers) from the continent of Antarctica.

The coastline of South America is fairly regular. It has no large bays, gulfs, or large peninsulas as do some of the other continents. A chain of rugged islands lies off southwestern Chile. In the extreme south, Tierra del Fuego is separated from the mainland by the Strait of Magellan. Other islands are the Falklands off southeastern Argentina and the Galapagos off Ecuador.

If you look at the map, you will notice that South America has two outstanding features—a series of high mountains running along the west coast and a great river stretching across the continent. A closer study will show you that the geographical features of South America are similar to those of North America in some ways. As North America, South America has highlands on the east coast and inland plains. But the two continents are not very much alike in climate and vegetation.

With the equator crossing South America near its broadest width, most of the continent lies in the tropics. In the lowland area of the Amazon it is hot and humid the year round. Temperatures get progressively cooler at higher elevations. But in South America, even at higher elevations, the temperatures are not very low. In fact, in the plateau areas of the mountains, thousands of feet above sea level, the Indians and Spaniards established large settlements. The temperatures to the south of the equator are more moderate. But even at the southernmost tip, the weather does not become extremely cold.

Rainfall varies from very heavy, exceeding 100 inches (254 centimeters) annually in parts of the rainforests, to very light along the west coast between northern Chile and northern Peru. The Atacama Desert here is one of the driest areas on earth. Rainfall has never been recorded in some places of this desert.

The Andes are part of the great cordillera, or line of mountains, that extends the entire length of North America. In South America they rise steeply from the Pacific in long ranges of snow-capped peaks and wide plateaus. In the north, the Andes spread out into three separate branches. Farther south, the Andes widen to as much as 400 miles (644 kilometers) in Bolivia and enclose a series of high and wide flat areas called the *Altiplano,* or the Bolivian Plateau. To the south the range narrows and lowers to form a single range. It extends off the southern coast of Chile in a ragged fringe of islands. Mt. Aconcagua in west-central Argentina near the Chilean border is the highest point in the Western Hemisphere. The Andes contain many volcanoes, many of which are still active.

In the eastern part of South America there are two areas of highlands that might be compared to the Appalachians of North America. In the north are the mostly unexplored Guiana Highlands. The Brazilian Highlands are in the east-central South America. Both highland regions have rounded hills and worn-down mountains. Around their edges are steep cliffs over which rivers fall and rush to the sea. These rough waters hinder transportation on the rivers but they are possible sources of water power. The Brazilian Highlands are rich in minerals, and the soil is fertile. It is one of South America's important farming, grazing, and industrial areas.

In southern Argentina the cold, windy, dry tableland of Patagonia resembles the Laurentian Plateau of Canada. It is used mainly to graze sheep.

There are grassy plains, or *Llanos,* in the north near the Orinoco River. In Paraguay and northern Argentina, is the *Gran Chaco,* an area of low bushes and trees and grasslands. The most fertile of South America's plains is the *Pampas* of Argentina, a luxuriant grassland and one of the world's great agricultural regions. The plains of South America are more walled in with mountains and highlands than those of North America. That makes them more difficult to reach.

The lowlands are crossed by rivers. The largest lowland area is drained by the Amazon, the second-largest river in the world, after the Nile. With its tributaries, it forms the largest river system in the world. The Amazon drains over one-third of the continent and carries more water than any other river. It is navigable for 2,300 miles (3,700 kilometers) from the Atlantic Ocean to Iquitos in Peru. There are very few major cities along the river. Off the Amazon, transportation is extremely difficult because the area is covered with *selvas*—dense rainforests. The Brazilian government is building a highway through Amazonas and bringing in settlers to develop the region.

Other important rivers of South America are the Río de la Plata, the São Francisco, and the Orinoco.

---

1. List the four main lowland areas of South America.
2. Why is the Amazon River called the largest river system in the world?
3. One country has two capital cities. What is the country? What are its capitals?

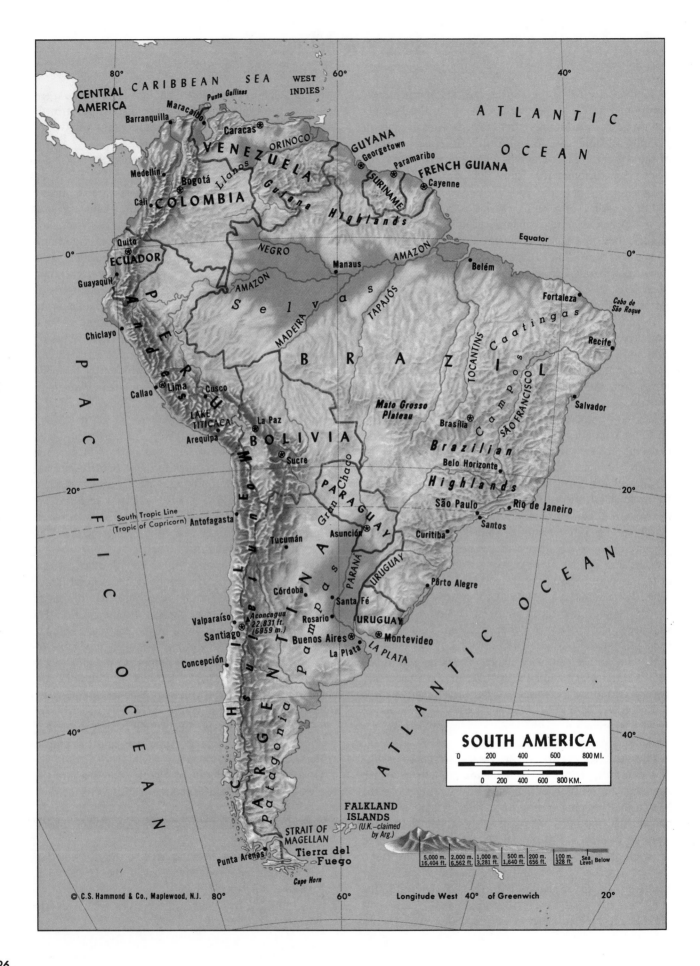

CENTRAL AMERICA
CARIBBEAN SEA
WEST INDIES
Punta Gallinas
ATLANTIC OCEAN

Barranquilla
Maracaibo
Caracas
VENEZUELA
ORINOCO
GUYANA
Georgetown
Paramaribo
SURINAME
FRENCH GUIANA
Cayenne

Medellín
Bogotá
Cali
COLOMBIA
Llanos
Guiana
Highlands

Quito
ECUADOR
Equator
0°

NEGRO
AMAZON
Manaus
AMAZON
Belém

Guayaquil
ANDES
AMAZON
Selvas
TAPAJÓS
Fortaleza
Cabo de São Roque

Chiclayo
PERU
Callao
Lima
Cusco
MADEIRA
BRAZIL
Recife
Caatingas
TOCANTINS

LAKE TITICACA
La Paz
Arequipa
BOLIVIA
Sucre
Mato Grosso Plateau
Brasília
Campos
SÃO FRANCISCO
Salvador

Chaco
PARAGUAY
Brazilian
Belo Horizonte
Highlands

South Tropic Line (Tropic of Capricorn)
Antofagasta
Gran
Mountains
São Paulo
Rio de Janeiro
20°

Tucumán
Asunción
PARAGUAY
Curitiba
Santos

PARANÁ
URUGUAY
Pôrto Alegre

Córdoba
ARGENTINA
Santa Fé
URUGUAY

Valparaíso
Aconcagua 22,831 ft. (6959 m.)
Rosario
Santiago
Buenos Aires
Montevideo
LA PLATA
La Plata

Concepción
Pampas

Patagonia
PARAGENTINA

40°

FALKLAND ISLANDS
(U.K.–claimed by Arg.)

STRAIT OF MAGELLAN
Punta Arenas
Tierra del Fuego

Cape Horn

© C.S. Hammond & Co., Maplewood, N.J.   80°   60°   Longitude West 40° of Greenwich   20°

SOUTH AMERICA

| 0 | 200 | 400 | 600 | 800 MI. |

| 0 | 200 | 400 | 600 | 800 KM. |

| 5,000 m. 16,404 ft. | 2,000 m. 6,562 ft. | 1,000 m. 3,281 ft. | 500 m. 1,640 ft. | 200 m. 656 ft. | 100 m. 328 ft. | Sea Level | Below |

PACIFIC OCEAN

ATLANTIC OCEAN

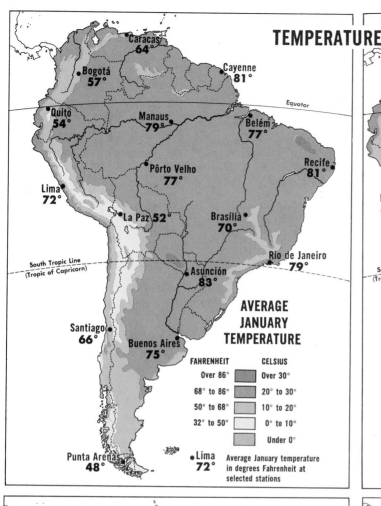

TEMPERATURE

AVERAGE JANUARY TEMPERATURE

Caracas 64°
Bogotá 57°
Cayenne 81°
Quito 54°
Manaus 79°
Belém 77°
Recife 81°
Lima 72°
La Paz 52°
Brasília 70°
Rio de Janeiro 79°
Asunción 83°
Santiago 66°
Buenos Aires 75°
Punta Arenas 48°

Equator
South Tropic Line (Tropic of Capricorn)

FAHRENHEIT	CELSIUS
Over 86°	Over 30°
68° to 86°	20° to 30°
50° to 68°	10° to 20°
32° to 50°	0° to 10°
	Under 0°

• Lima 72° — Average January temperature in degrees Fahrenheit at selected stations

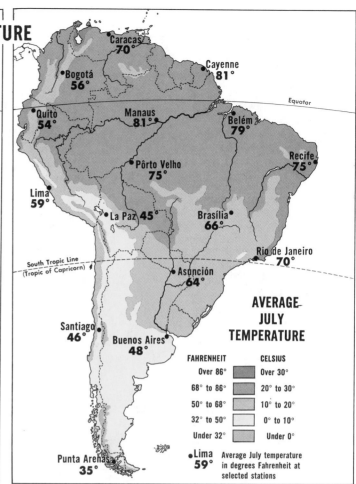

AVERAGE JULY TEMPERATURE

Caracas 70°
Bogotá 56°
Cayenne 81°
Quito 54°
Manaus 81°
Belém 79°
Recife 75°
Lima 59°
La Paz 45°
Brasília 66°
Rio de Janeiro 70°
Asunción 64°
Santiago 46°
Buenos Aires 48°
Punta Arenas 35°

Equator
South Tropic Line (Tropic of Capricorn)

FAHRENHEIT	CELSIUS
Over 86°	Over 30°
68° to 86°	20° to 30°
50° to 68°	10° to 20°
32° to 50°	0° to 10°
Under 32°	Under 0°

• Lima 59° — Average July temperature in degrees Fahrenheit at selected stations

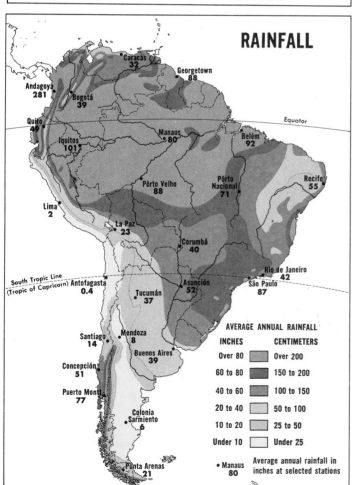

RAINFALL

Caracas 32
Georgetown 88
Andagoyá 281
Bogotá 39
Quito 49
Iquitos 101
Manaus 80
Belém 92
Pôrto Velho 88
Pôrto Nacional 71
Recife 55
Lima 2
La Paz 23
Corumbá 40
Rio de Janeiro 42
Antofagasta 0.4
Tucumán 37
Asunción 52
São Paulo 87
Santiago 14
Mendoza 8
Buenos Aires 39
Concepción 51
Puerto Montt 77
Colonia Sarmiento 6
Punta Arenas 21

Equator
South Tropic Line (Tropic of Capricorn)

AVERAGE ANNUAL RAINFALL

INCHES	CENTIMETERS
Over 80	Over 200
60 to 80	150 to 200
40 to 60	100 to 150
20 to 40	50 to 100
10 to 20	25 to 50
Under 10	Under 25

• Manaus 80 — Average annual rainfall in inches at selected stations

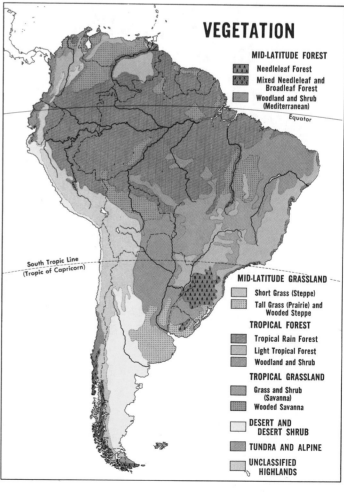

VEGETATION

MID-LATITUDE FOREST
- Needleleaf Forest
- Mixed Needleleaf and Broadleaf Forest
- Woodland and Shrub (Mediterranean)

MID-LATITUDE GRASSLAND
- Short Grass (Steppe)
- Tall Grass (Prairie) and Wooded Steppe

TROPICAL FOREST
- Tropical Rain Forest
- Light Tropical Forest
- Woodland and Shrub

TROPICAL GRASSLAND
- Grass and Shrub (Savanna)
- Wooded Savanna

- DESERT AND DESERT SHRUB
- TUNDRA AND ALPINE
- UNCLASSIFIED HIGHLANDS

Equator
South Tropic Line (Tropic of Capricorn)

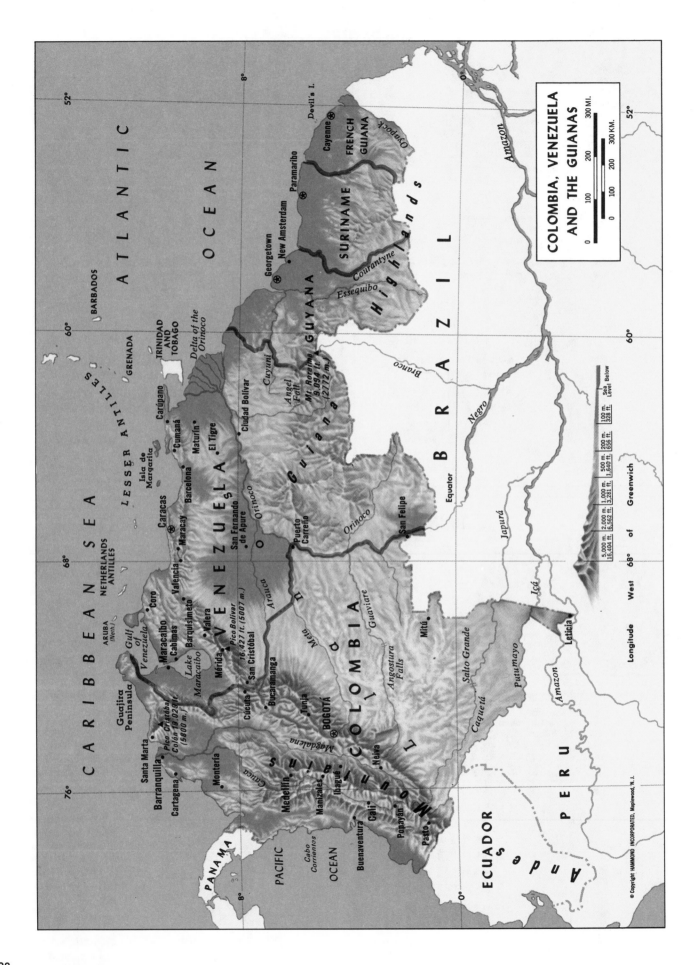

COLOMBIA, VENEZUELA
AND THE GUIANAS

300 MI.
200
100
300 KM.
200
100
0
0

ATLANTIC

OCEAN

Devil's I.

Cayenne ⊛

FRENCH
GUIANA

Oyapock

Amazon

Paramaribo ⊛

SURINAME

New Amsterdam

Guiana

Highlands

BARBADOS

Georgetown ⊛

GUYANA

Courantyne

Essequibo

CARIBBEAN SEA

LESSER ANTILLES

GRENADA

TRINIDAD
AND
TOBAGO

Delta of the
Orinoco

Cuyuni

Angel
Fall

Mt. Roraima
9,094 ft.
(2772 m.)

BRAZIL

Branco

Carúpano

Isla de
Margarita

Cumaná

Maturín

Barcelona

El Tigre

Ciudad Bolívar

Negro

Caracas ⊛

Maracay

Valencia

V E N E Z U E L A

San Fernando
de Apure

Orinoco

G
u
i
a
n
a

Orinoco

San Felipe

Equator

Japurá

ARUBA
(Neth.)

NETHERLANDS
ANTILLES

Coro

Barquisimeto

Pico Bolívar
16,427 ft. (5007 m.)

Arauca

Meta

Puerto
Carreño

Guaviare

Icá

Gulf of
Venezuela

Maracaibo

Cabimas

Valera

Mérida

San Cristóbal

O
R
I
N
O
C
O

Mitú

Salto Grande

Lake
Maracaibo

Cúcuta

Bucaramanga

Tunja

BOGOTÁ ⊛

C O L O M B I A

Angostura
Falls

Caquetá

Putumayo

Leticia

Guajira
Peninsula

Santa Marta

Pico Cristóbal
Colón 19,029 ft.
(5800 m.)

Magdalena

Neiva

Amazon

Barranquilla

Cartagena

Montería

Cauca

Medellín

Manizales

Ibagué

M
o
u
n
t
a
i
n
s

Cali

Popayán

Pasto

PERU

PACIFIC

Cabo
Corrientes

OCEAN

Buenaventura

ECUADOR

A
n
d
e
s

5,000 m. 2,000 m. 1,000 m. 500 m. 200 m. 100 m. Sea Below
16,404 ft. 6,562 ft. 3,281 ft. 1,640 ft. 656 ft. 328 ft. Level

PANAMA

76°

68°

60°

52°

8°

8°

0°

Longitude   West   68°   of   Greenwich   60°

© Copyright HAMMOND INCORPORATED, Maplewood, N.J.

28

PERU and ECUADOR

Esmeraldas
Tulcán
Ibarra
Quito ⊛
Cotopaxi
▲ 19,347 ft. (5897 m.)

E C U A D O R

Cabo
San Lorenzo
Manta
Chimborazo
20,561 ft.
(6267 m.)
Ambato
Riobamba
Guayaquil

Gulf of
Guayaquil
Cuenca
Tumbes
Machala
Loja

Talara
Chira
Piura
Punta Aguja

C O L O M B I A

Equator

Napo
Putumayo
Içá

Pastaza

Iquitos
Amazon
Marañón
Yavarí

B R A Z I L

Yurimaguas
Tarapoto
Ucayali
Juruá

Chiclayo
Cajamarca
Marañón

P E R U

Trujillo
Chimbote
Huascarán
▲ 22,205 ft.
(6768 m.)
Huarás

M o n t a ñ a

Purus

Huánuco
Cerro de Pasco
Huacho
La Oroya
LIMA ⊛
Callao ⊛
Huancayo
Huancavelica
Ayacucho
Pisco
Ica

Madre de Dios
Puerto Maldonado

Apurímac
Cusco
Sicuani
▲ Vilcanota
17,999 ft.
(5486 m.)
Juliaca
Lake
Titicaca
Puno

B O L I V I A

El Misti
19,101 ft. ▲
(5822 m.)
Arequipa
Altiplano

Tacna
C H I L E

P A C I F I C

O C E A N

5,000 m. | 2,000 m. | 1,000 m. | 500 m. | 200 m. | 100 m. | Sea
16,404 ft. | 6,562 ft. | 3,281 ft. | 1,640 ft. | 656 ft. | 328 ft. | Level | Below

0 50 100   200   300 MI.
0 50 100   200   300 KM.

© Copyright HAMMOND INCORPORATED, Maplewood, N.J.

76° Longitude West of Greenwich 72°

29

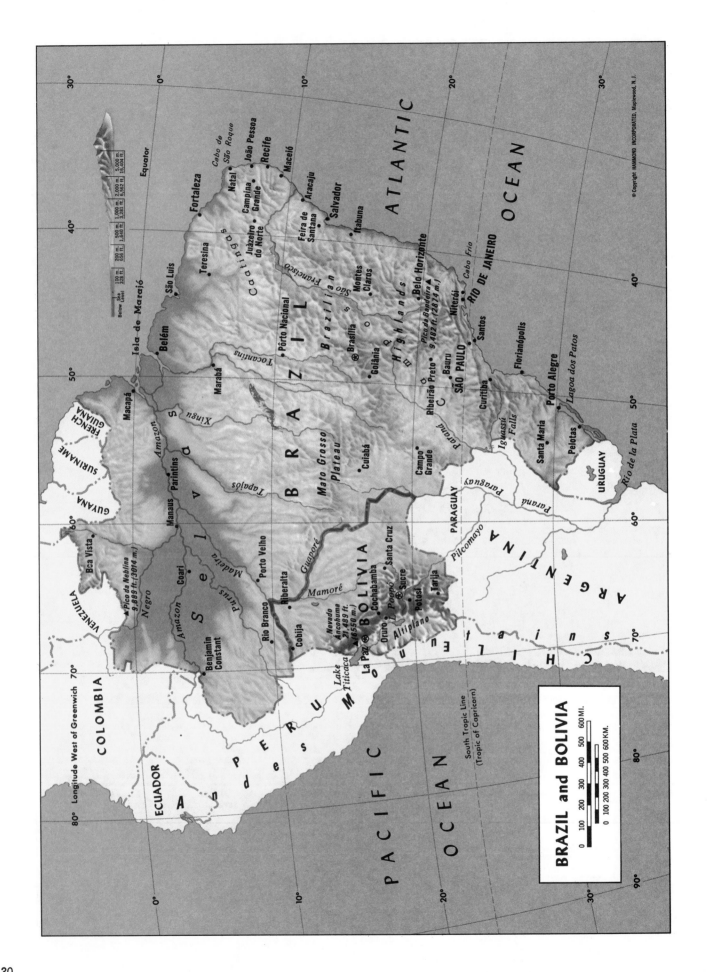

BRAZIL and BOLIVIA

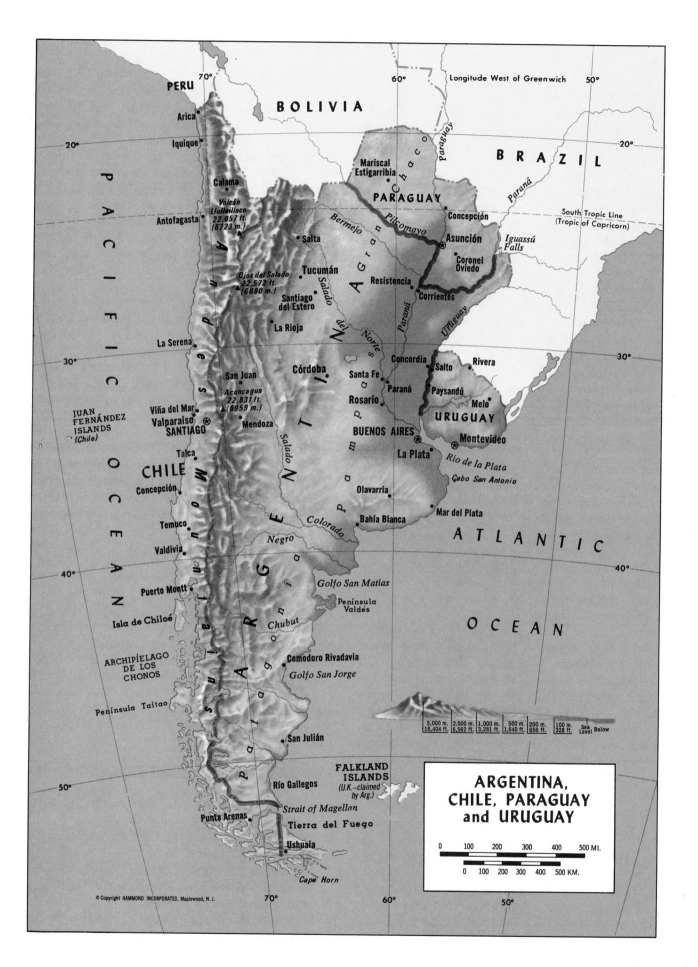

PERU

BOLIVIA

BRAZIL

Longitude West of Greenwich

70° 60° 50°

20° 20°

Arica

Iquique

P A C I F I C   O C E A N

Calama

Volcán
Llullaillaco
22,057 ft.
(6723 m.)

Antofagasta

Mariscal
Estigarribia

Chaco

PARAGUAY

Paraguay

Concepción

South Tropic Line
(Tropic of Capricorn)

Asunción

Iguassú
Falls

Salta

Bermejo

Pilcomayo

Coronel
Oviedo

Ojos del Salado
22,572 ft.
(6880 m.)

Tucumán

Resistencia

Corrientes

Salado

Santiago
del Estero

Paraná

Uruguay

La Rioja

Norte

Concordia

Rivera

30° La Serena 30°

San Juan

Córdoba

Salto

JUAN
FERNÁNDEZ
ISLANDS
(Chile)

Aconcagua
22,831 ft.
(6959 m.)

Santa Fe

Paysandú

Viña del Mar
Valparaíso
SANTIAGO

Mendoza

Paraná

Rosario

Melo

Salado

URUGUAY

Talca

BUENOS AIRES

Montevideo

CHILE

La Plata

Río de la Plata

Concepción

Olavarría

Cabo San Antonio

Temuco

Bahía Blanca

Mar del Plata

A T L A N T I C

Valdivia

Colorado

40° Negro 40°

Puerto Montt

Golfo San Matías

Isla de Chiloé

Península
Valdés

O C E A N

Chubut

ARCHIPÍELAGO
DE LOS
CHONOS

Comodoro Rivadavia

Golfo San Jorge

Península Taitao

San Julián

5,000 m.   2,000 m.   1,000 m.   500 m.   200 m.   100 m.   Sea
16,404 ft.   6,562 ft.   3,281 ft.   1,640 ft.   656 ft.   328 ft.   Level   Below

FALKLAND
ISLANDS
(U.K.–claimed
by Arg.)

Río Gallegos

50° 50°

Strait of Magellan

Punta Arenas

Tierra del Fuego

Ushuaia

© Copyright HAMMOND INCORPORATED, Maplewood, N.J.

70° 60° 50°

Cape Horn

ARGENTINA,
CHILE, PARAGUAY
and URUGUAY

0   100   200   300   400   500 MI.

0   100   200   300   400   500 KM.

AFRICA

Africa, the second largest continent, is cut almost in half by the equator. Because the bulge of land in western Africa is so large, most of Africa lies in the Northern Hemisphere.

For the most part, Africa has a smooth coastline. There are no large bays or deep inlets to form natural harbors. The majority of Africa's seaports are in the north along the Mediterranean Sea.

Africa does not have a great many islands lying off its coasts. Madagascar, the fourth largest island in the world, is off the southeast coast. Many of Africa's islands are independent countries.

Most of Africa is a high plateau. Its height ranges between 2,000 feet (610 meters) and 5,000 feet (1,524 meters) above sea level. This tableland is lower in the north and west and higher in the south and east. It is almost surrounded by a narrow, coastal plain.

Various parts of Africa have different climates, depending on rainfall and elevation. In North Africa, for example, where there is very little rain, the plateau has a desert climate. Around the equator the rainfall is heavy and there are periods of torrential rain. The low plateaus in this area are covered with dense rainforests, and it is always hot and humid. In the equatorial regions in the east where the land is higher, the temperatures are lower and there are extensive grasslands. In general, the climate is cooler in areas of higher elevation and in the northern and southern parts of the continent. In South Africa, the temperate climate and lack of dense rainforests have made it easier for people there to develop the region's rich mineral resources.

The most outstanding feature of Africa by far is the Sahara desert. It covers an area larger than the United States and stretches southward from the Atlas Mountains and westward from the Atlantic Ocean to the Red Sea across a distance of about 3,200 miles (5,150 kilometers). The Sahara is a dry region that supports little life. Some parts have shifting sand dunes (ergs). Other parts are covered with pebbles. And still other sections are bare rocky plains. Among the desert's highlands are the Ahaggar of Algeria, the Tibesti of Chad and Libya, and the Aïr of Niger. In the east the Sahara is made up of a number of smaller deserts—the Libyan, Arabian, and Nubian deserts.

The desert has a number of shallow streams and rivers during periods of rainfall. These rivers do not reach the coast and usually peter out in the sand. Only the Nile carries a large enough volume of water to reach the sea all the time. From its sources in Lake Tana and Lake Victoria, the Nile flows northward for over 4,100 miles (6,600 kilometers) into the Mediterranean Sea.

With its seasonal flooding, the Nile turns the surrounding land into a fertile valley. Oases can be found scattered throughout the Sahara. Their water comes from springs and wells. Other deserts of Africa are the Kalahari and the Great Karoo in the south. The Sahara is the dividing line between the Arab nations to the north and the mainly Black nations to the south.

In the northwest corner of the continent and paralleling the coast are the rugged Atlas Mountains. They are a continuation of the Alpine system of southern Europe, and they have some plateau regions within them. These mountains separate the northwest coastal plain from the Sahara.

The main mountain range in southeastern Africa is the Drakensberg. It lies between Swaziland and Lesotho. North of the Drakensberg are a series of highlands and plateaus that extend northward to the Red Sea. This region is the highest part of the continent, and the Ethiopian Highlands form its highest section.

Running through these eastern highlands from Ethiopia southwards to Mozambique is a long depression, or opening in the earth, known as the Great Rift Valley. Actually it begins in Syria and runs under the Red Sea to northeastern Ethiopia. Long ago, huge cracks occurred in the earth, and the land in between the cracks sank to form a series of valleys. Almost all of the lakes in east Africa are part of the rift. Only Lake Victoria, Africa's largest lake, is not. The highest mountains of Africa are towering volcanic peaks that lie near the rift valleys. They include Mt. Kilimanjaro in Tanzania, which is the highest mountain in Africa, and Mt. Kenya in Kenya. The lava from volcanoes in this area have given much of it very fertile soil. In the past, the Great Rift Valley prevented the development of extensive communication between the east and west.

Africa has a number of long rivers besides the Nile. They include the Congo (Zaire), the Niger, Orange, and Zambezi. Many of Africa's rivers have rapids and waterfalls, which are obstacles to transportation. Some have sandbars at the mouth or low water levels during part of the year.

1. Two countries have capital cities on the Nile River. Name the countries and their capitals.
2. What important waterway links the Mediterranean Sea with the Red Sea?
3. List the countries that lie entirely between the equator and the South Tropic line (Tropic of Capricorn).
4. What is the Great Rift Valley?
5. What five countries share waters of the Niger River?

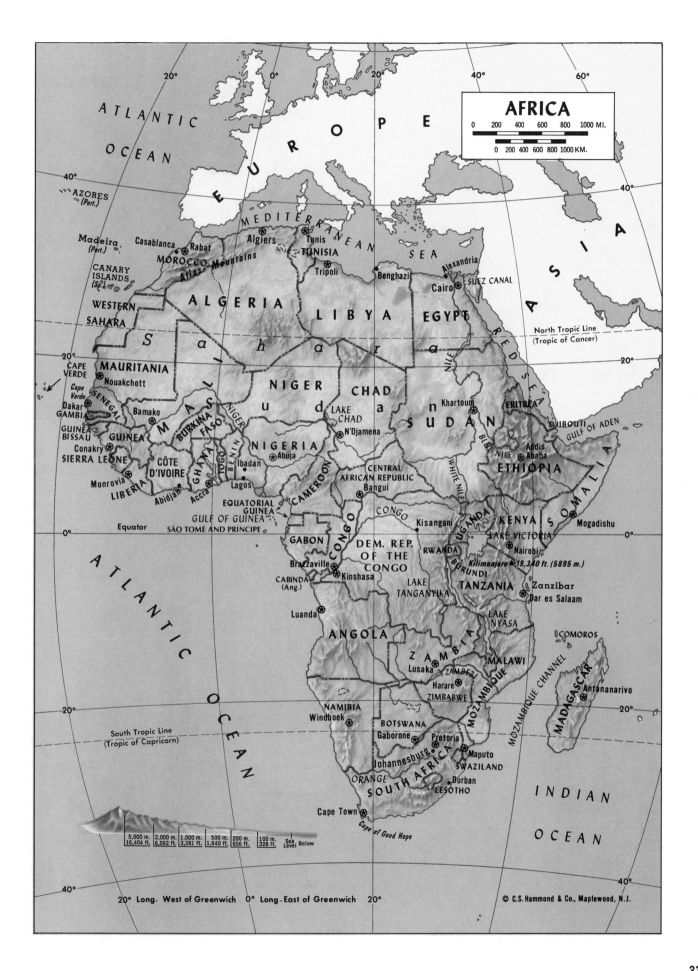

ATLANTIC
OCEAN

EUROPE

ASIA

AZORES
(Port.)

Madeira
(Port.)

Casablanca • Rabat   Algiers   Tunis
MOROCCO • Atlas Mountains   TUNISIA
CANARY   Atlas Mountains   Tripoli   Benghazi
ISLANDS   (Sp.)

WESTERN   ALGERIA   LIBYA   EGYPT
SAHARA   Suez Canal
                                          Cairo
CAPE   MAURITANIA   North Tropic Line
VERDE   • Nouakchott   (Tropic of Cancer)
Cape   S   a   h   a   r   a
Verde
Dakar   SENEGAL
GAMBIA   Bamako
GUINEA-   BURKINA   NIGER   CHAD   Khartoum   ERITREA
BISSAU   Conakry   FASO   LAKE   N'Djamena   DJIBOUTI   GULF OF ADEN
SIERRA LEONE   GHANA   NIGERIA   CHAD   SUDAN   Addis   GULF OF ADEN
                    CÔTE   TOGO   Abuja   Ababa
Monrovia   D'IVOIRE   Ibadan   CAMEROON   CENTRAL   ETHIOPIA   Mogadishu
LIBERIA   Abidjan   Accra   Lagos   AFRICAN REPUBLIC   WHITE NILE
            EQUATORIAL   Bangui   UGANDA   KENYA   SOMALIA
Equator   GUINEA   GULF OF GUINEA   CONGO   Kisangani   LAKE VICTORIA
            SÃO TOMÉ AND PRÍNCIPE   GABON   DEM. REP.   RWANDA   Nairobi
                                    OF THE   BURUNDI   Kilimanjaro – 19,340 ft. (5895 m.)
ATLANTIC   Brazzaville   CONGO   LAKE   TANZANIA   Zanzibar
            CABINDA   Kinshasa   TANGANYIKA   Dar es Salaam
            (Ang.)
            Luanda   LAKE   COMOROS
                        NYASA
OCEAN   ANGOLA   ZAMBIA   MALAWI
                        Lusaka   MOZAMBIQUE
                        ZAMBEZI   Antananarivo
South Tropic Line   NAMIBIA   Harare   MOZAMBIQUE CHANNEL   MADAGASCAR
(Tropic of Capricorn)   Windhoek   ZIMBABWE
            BOTSWANA   Maputo
            Gaborone   Pretoria   SWAZILAND
            Johannesburg   SOUTH AFRICA
            ORANGE   Durban
            SOUTH AFRICA   LESOTHO   INDIAN
            Cape Town
            Cape of Good Hope   OCEAN

5,000 m.   2,000 m.   1,000 m.   500 m.   200 m.   100 m.   Sea
16,404 ft.   6,562 ft.   3,281 ft.   1,640 ft.   656 ft.   328 ft.   Level   Below

20° Long. West of Greenwich   0° Long. East of Greenwich   20°   © C.S. Hammond & Co., Maplewood, N.J.

AFRICA
0   200   400   600   800   1000 MI.
0   200 400 600 800 1000 KM.

TEMPERATURE

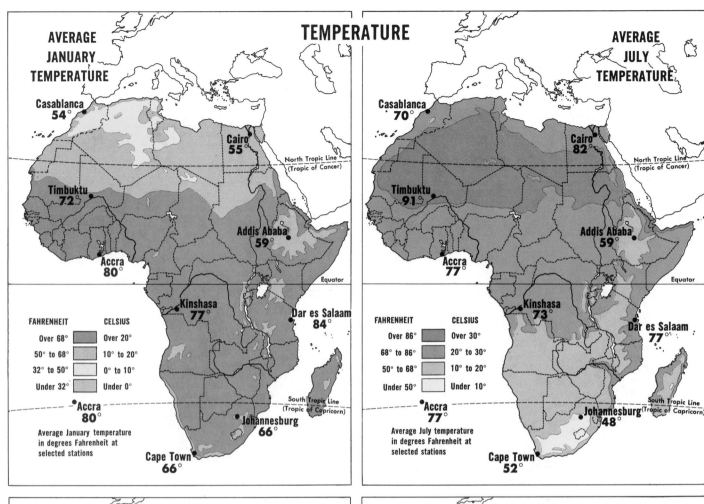

AVERAGE JANUARY TEMPERATURE

- Casablanca 54°
- Cairo 55°
- Timbuktu 72°
- Addis Ababa 59°
- Accra 80°
- Kinshasa 77°
- Dar es Salaam 84°
- Johannesburg 66°
- Cape Town 66°

North Tropic Line (Tropic of Cancer)

Equator

South Tropic Line (Tropic of Capricorn)

FAHRENHEIT	CELSIUS
Over 68°	Over 20°
50° to 68°	10° to 20°
32° to 50°	0° to 10°
Under 32°	Under 0°

● Accra 80°

Average January temperature in degrees Fahrenheit at selected stations

AVERAGE JULY TEMPERATURE

- Casablanca 70°
- Cairo 82°
- Timbuktu 91°
- Addis Ababa 59°
- Accra 77°
- Kinshasa 73°
- Dar es Salaam 77°
- Johannesburg 48°
- Cape Town 52°

North Tropic Line (Tropic of Cancer)

Equator

South Tropic Line (Tropic of Capricorn)

FAHRENHEIT	CELSIUS
Over 86°	Over 30°
68° to 86°	20° to 30°
50° to 68°	10° to 20°
Under 50°	Under 10°

● Accra 77°

Average July temperature in degrees Fahrenheit at selected stations

RAINFALL

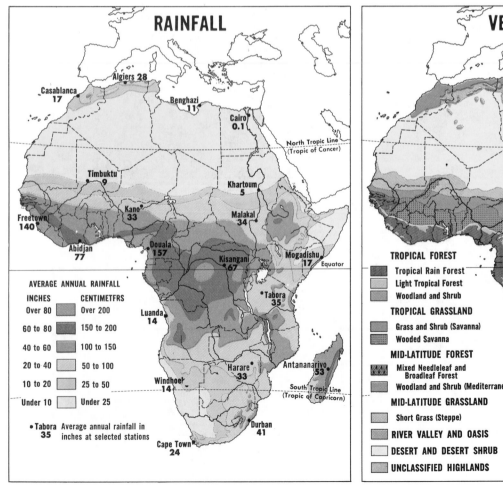

- Algiers 28
- Casablanca 17
- Benghazi 11
- Cairo 0.1
- Timbuktu 9
- Khartoum 5
- Kano 33
- Malakal 34
- Freetown 140
- Abidjan 77
- Douala 157
- Kisangani 67
- Mogadishu 17
- Tabora 35
- Luanda 14
- Harare 33
- Antananarivo 53
- Windhoek 14
- Durban 41
- Cape Town 24

North Tropic Line (Tropic of Cancer)

Equator

South Tropic Line (Tropic of Capricorn)

AVERAGE ANNUAL RAINFALL

INCHES	CENTIMETERS
Over 80	Over 200
60 to 80	150 to 200
40 to 60	100 to 150
20 to 40	50 to 100
10 to 20	25 to 50
Under 10	Under 25

● Tabora 35 — Average annual rainfall in inches at selected stations

VEGETATION

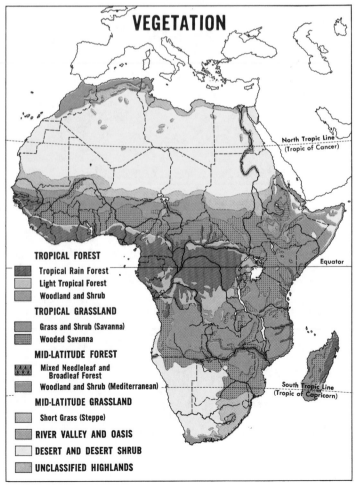

North Tropic Line (Tropic of Cancer)

Equator

South Tropic Line (Tropic of Capricorn)

TROPICAL FOREST
- Tropical Rain Forest
- Light Tropical Forest
- Woodland and Shrub

TROPICAL GRASSLAND
- Grass and Shrub (Savanna)
- Wooded Savanna

MID-LATITUDE FOREST
- Mixed Needleleaf and Broadleaf Forest
- Woodland and Shrub (Mediterranean)

MID-LATITUDE GRASSLAND
- Short Grass (Steppe)

RIVER VALLEY AND OASIS

DESERT AND DESERT SHRUB

UNCLASSIFIED HIGHLANDS

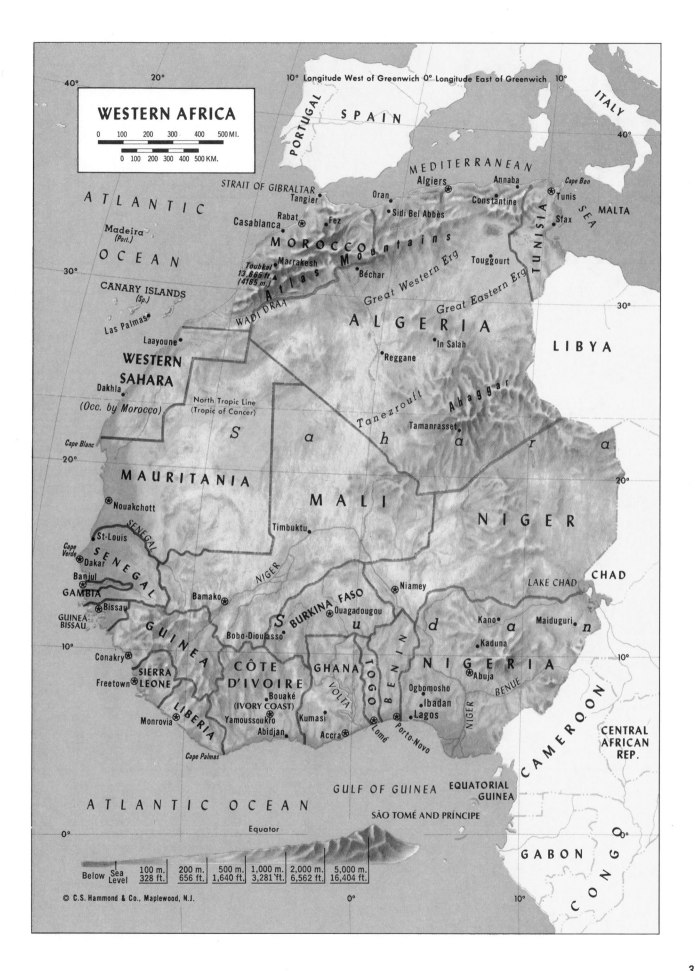

WESTERN AFRICA

0 100 200 300 400 500 MI.

0 100 200 300 400 500 KM.

40°
20°
10° Longitude West of Greenwich 0° Longitude East of Greenwich 10°

ITALY

PORTUGAL
SPAIN
40°

MEDITERRANEAN

A T L A N T I C

STRAIT OF GIBRALTAR
Tangier
Oran
Algiers ⊗
Annaba
Cape Bon
Tunis ⊗
SEA
MALTA

Madeira
(Port.)
Casablanca
Rabat ⊗
Fez
Sidi Bel Abbès
Constantine
TUNISIA
Sfax

O C E A N
MOROCCO tains
Marrakesh
Béchar
Touggourt

30°
CANARY ISLANDS
(Sp.)
Toubkal
13,665 ft.▲
(4165 m.)
Atlas Mountains
Great Western Erg
Great Eastern Erg
30°

Las Palmas
WADI DRAA
A L G E R I A
LIBYA

Laayoune
In Salah
Reggane

WESTERN
SAHARA
North Tropic Line
(Tropic of Cancer)
S
a
h
Tanezrouft
Ahaggar
a
r
a

Dakhla
Tamanrasset

(Occ. by Morocco)

Cape Blanc
20°
20°

M A U R I T A N I A
M A L I
N I G E R
20°

Nouakchott ⊗
LAKE CHAD
CHAD

St-Louis
SENEGAL
Timbuktu
NIGER

Cape
Verde
Dakar ⊗
SENEGAL
Niamey ⊗
Kano
Maiduguri

Banjul
GAMBIA
Bamako ⊗
S
BURKINA FASO
u
d
a
Kaduna
n

Bissau ⊗
GUINEA-
BISSAU
GUINEA
Bobo-Dioulasso
Ouagadougou ⊗
N I G E R I A

10°
Conakry ⊗
CÔTE
D'IVOIRE
(IVORY COAST)
GHANA
VOLTA
TOGO
BENIN
Ogbomosho
Ibadan
Abuja ⊗
10°

Freetown ⊗
SIERRA
LEONE
Bouaké
Lagos

LIBERIA
Yamoussoukro
Kumasi
Lomé
Porto-Novo
BENUE

Monrovia ⊗
Abidjan
Accra ⊗
NIGER

Cape Palmas
CAMEROON
CENTRAL
AFRICAN
REP.

A T L A N T I C   O C E A N
GULF OF GUINEA
EQUATORIAL
GUINEA

SÃO TOMÉ AND PRÍNCIPE

0°
Equator
GABON
CONGO
0°

Below Sea
Level
100 m.
328 ft.
200 m.
656 ft.
500 m.
1,640 ft.
1,000 m.
3,281 ft.
2,000 m.
6,562 ft.
5,000 m.
16,404 ft.

© C.S. Hammond & Co., Maplewood, N.J.

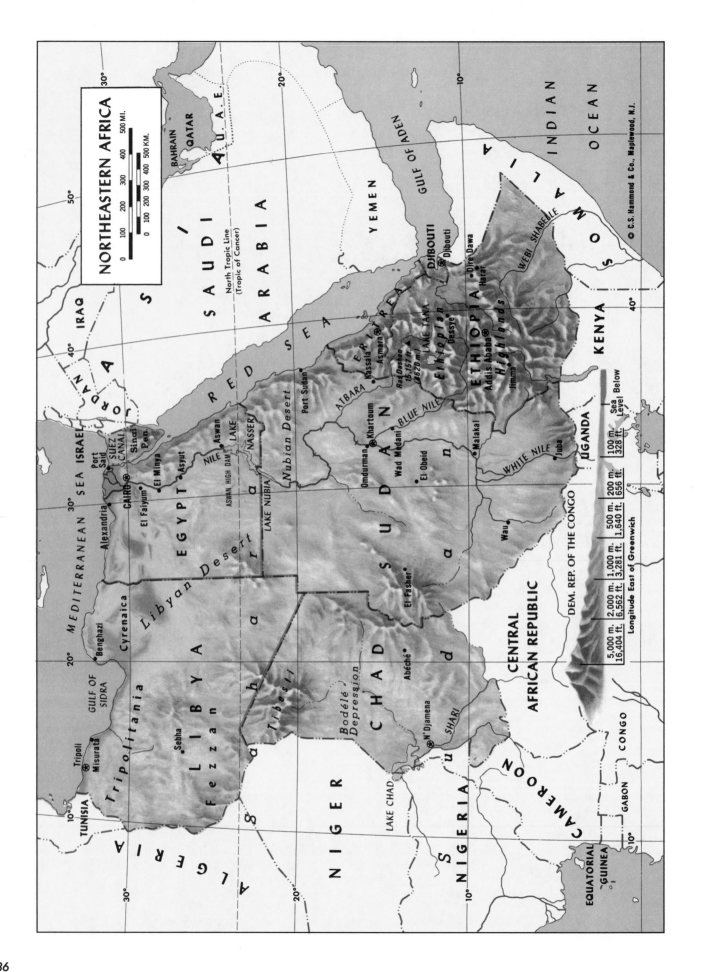

NORTHEASTERN AFRICA

500 MI.

400

300

200

100

0

500 KM.

400

300

200

100

0

North Tropic Line
(Tropic of Cancer)

© C.S. Hammond & Co., Maplewood, N.J.

IRAQ

JORDAN

ISRAEL

SINAI Pen.

SUEZ CANAL

Port Said

Alexandria

CAIRO

El Minya

El Faiyum

Asyut

EGYPT

NILE

Aswan

ASWAN HIGH DAM

LAKE NASSER

LAKE NUBIA

Libyan Desert

Cyrenaica

Benghazi

GULF OF SIDRA

Tripolitania

Tripoli

Misurata

TUNISIA

ALGERIA

LIBYA

Sebha

Fezzan

Tibesti

Bodélé Depression

Sahara

Abéché

CHAD

N'Djamena

SHARI

LAKE CHAD

NIGER

NIGERIA

CAMEROON

EQUATORIAL GUINEA

GABON

CONGO

DEM. REP. OF THE CONGO

CENTRAL AFRICAN REPUBLIC

MEDITERRANEAN SEA

SAUDI ARABIA

BAHRAIN

QATAR

U.A.E.

OMAN

RED SEA

Nubian Desert

Port Sudan

Sahara

SUDAN

El Fasher

El Obeid

Wau

Malakal

Wad Medani

Omdurman

Khartoum

ATBARA

Kassala

Asmara

ERITREA

YEMEN

GULF OF ADEN

DJIBOUTI

Djibouti

Dire Dawa

Harar

WEBI SHABELLE

SOMALIA

INDIAN OCEAN

Ras Dashan
15,157 ft.
(4620 m.)

LAKE TANA

BLUE NILE

Dessye

Ethiopian Highlands

Addis Ababa

Jimma

ETHIOPIA

WHITE NILE

Juba

UGANDA

KENYA

Longitude East of Greenwich

| 5,000 m. | 2,000 m. | 1,000 m. | 500 m. | 200 m. | 100 m. | Sea Level Below |
| 16,404 ft. | 6,562 ft. | 3,281 ft. | 1,640 ft. | 656 ft. | 328 ft. | |

36

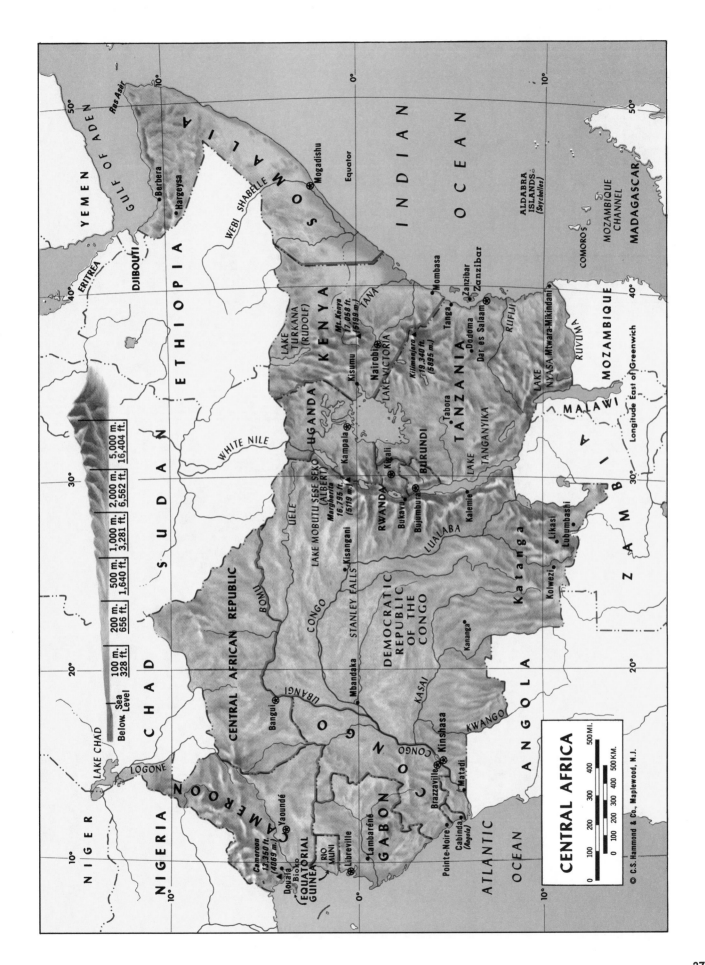

CENTRAL AFRICA

© C.S. Hammond & Co., Maplewood, N.J.

5,000 m. 16,404 ft.
2,000 m. 6,562 ft.
1,000 m. 3,281 ft.
500 m. 1,640 ft.
200 m. 656 ft.
100 m. 328 ft.
Sea Level
Below Sea Level

YEMEN

GULF OF ADEN

ERITREA

DJIBOUTI

ETHIOPIA

S O M A L I A

Ras Asér

Berbera
Hargeysa

Mogadishu

WEBI SHABELLE

INDIAN OCEAN

Equator

ALDABRA ISLANDS (Seychelles)

COMOROS

MOZAMBIQUE CHANNEL

MADAGASCAR

SUDAN

WHITE NILE

CHAD

LAKE CHAD

LOGONE

NIGER

NIGERIA

CAMEROON

Cameroon 13,350 ft. (4069 m.)

Bioko

Douala
Yaoundé

EQUATORIAL GUINEA

RIO MUNI

Libreville

Lambaréné

GABON

Pointe-Noire

Cabinda (Angola)

CONGO

Brazzaville

Matadi

Kinshasa

ATLANTIC OCEAN

ANGOLA

KWANGO

Kananga

KASAI

CENTRAL AFRICAN REPUBLIC

BOMU

UELE

UBANGI

Bangui

CONGO

STANLEY FALLS

Mbandaka

DEMOCRATIC REPUBLIC OF THE CONGO

Kisangani

LAKE MOBUTU SESE SEKO (ALBERT)

Margherita 16,795 ft. (5119 m.)

UGANDA

Kampala

LAKE TURKANA (RUDOLF)

KENYA

Mt. Kenya 17,058 ft. (5199 m.)

TANA

Kisumu

Nairobi

LAKE VICTORIA

RWANDA

Kigali

BURUNDI

Bukavu

Bujumbura

LUALABA

Kilimanjaro 19,340 ft. (5895 m.)

TANZANIA

Tabora

Dodoma

Dar es Salaam

RUFIJI

Mombasa

Tanga

Zanzibar

LAKE TANGANYIKA

Kalemie

Katanga

Likasi

Lubumbashi

Kolwezi

ZAMBIA

LAKE NYASA

MALAWI

MOZAMBIQUE

RUVUMA

Mtwara-Mikindani

Longitude East of Greenwich

CENTRAL AFRICA

500 MI.
100 200 300 400
0 100 200 300 400 500 KM.

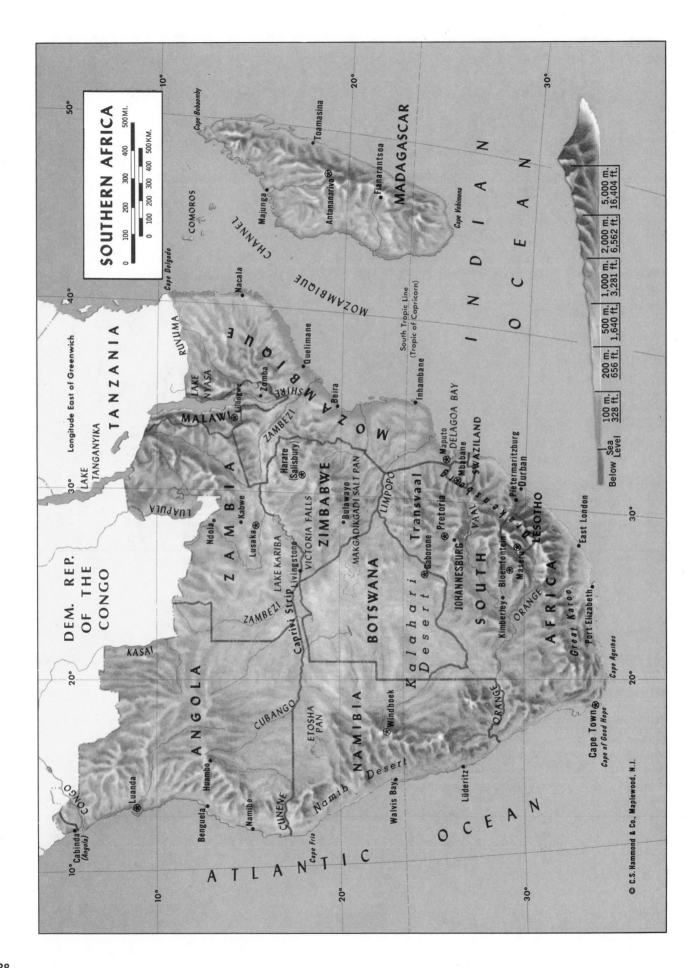

SOUTHERN AFRICA

500 MI.
400
300
200
100
0

500 KM.
400
300
200
100
0

5,000 m.
16,404 ft.

2,000 m.
6,562 ft.

1,000 m.
3,281 ft.

500 m.
1,640 ft.

200 m.
656 ft.

100 m.
328 ft.

Sea
Level

Below
Sea Level

INDIAN OCEAN

MADAGASCAR

Toamasina
Fianarantsoa
Antananarivo
Majunga
Cape Vohimena

COMOROS
Cape Bobaomby
Cape Delgado

MOZAMBIQUE CHANNEL

Nacala
Quelimane
Zomba
Beira
Inhambane

DELAGOA BAY
Maputo
Mbabane
SWAZILAND
Pietermaritzburg
Durban

South Tropic Line
(Tropic of Capricorn)

TANZANIA
Longitude East of Greenwich

LAKE TANGANYIKA

LAKE NYASA
MALAWI
Lilongwe
ZAMBEZI

RUVUMA
SHIRE
MOZAMBIQUE

ZAMBIA
Ndola
Kabwe
Lusaka
LUAPULA

Harare (Salisbury)
ZIMBABWE
Bulawayo
MAKGADIKGADI SALT PAN
VICTORIA FALLS
LAKE KARIBA
Livingstone
Caprivi Strip
ZAMBEZI

LIMPOPO
Transvaal
Gaborone
Pretoria
JOHANNESBURG
VAAL
SOUTH
Bloemfontein
Kimberley
Maseru
LESOTHO
ORANGE
AFRICA
East London
Great Karoo
Port Elizabeth

DEM. REP. OF THE CONGO
KASAI
CONGO

ANGOLA
Luanda
Huambo
Benguela
Namibe
Cabinda (Angola)
CUNENE

CUBANGO
ETOSHA PAN
NAMIBIA
Windhoek
Namib Desert
Walvis Bay
Cape Fria
Lüderitz

BOTSWANA
Kalahari Desert

ORANGE
Cape Town
Cape of Good Hope
Cape Agulhas

ATLANTIC OCEAN

50°
40°
30°
20°
10°
10°
20°
30°

10°
20°
30°

EUROPE

Europe is the second-smallest continent. Only Australia is smaller. If you look at the map, you will notice that you cannot tell from the shape where Europe ends and Asia begins. That is because there is no natural boundary between the two. Europe and Asia make up a large landmass known as Eurasia. People have traditionally drawn the boundary between the two along the Ural Mountains and Ural River to the Caspian Sea, and then westward along the border of Azerbaijan and Armenia to the Black Sea.

Europe is well shaped and situated for the development of sea trade. It has a very irregular shape. The number of large inlets of the ocean and of large peninsulas—and the fact that Europe itself is really a very large peninsula of Asia—means that no part of Europe is very far from the sea. Many places along its very indented coastline are natural harbors, and many of them are at the mouths of long rivers that run into the continent. Find the Thames, Rhine, Elbe, Seine, and the Tagus on the maps.

In the north, near the North and Baltic Seas, are the Scandinavian and Jutland peninsulas. Norway and Sweden occupy Scandinavia, and Denmark is on Jutland. Finland is often considered part of Scandinavia although it is not actually on the peninsula. To the southwest is the Iberian Peninsula on which Spain and Portugal are located. Italy thrusts into the Mediterranean Sea and the Balkan Peninsula is to its east. Study the positions of the peninsulas along the North Atlantic Ocean and the Mediterranean. Both bodies of water are major highways of world trade. Ships constantly cross the Atlantic to North and South America. Those bound for Asia sail across the Mediterranean and through the Suez Canal and the Red Sea to the east.

Many large islands and island groups are off the coast. The largest are the British Isles, which include Ireland. These islands are in the same latitude as Labrador in North America, but they have a much milder climate because the water and winds in the eastern Atlantic are warm. Farther out in the Atlantic is the island of Iceland, Europe's westernmost nation. Other large islands are in the Mediterranean Sea.

Europe has few areas that have not been cultivated or where people have not settled. Few areas do not have mineral resources. Coal and iron are important.

Europe has four major regions. They are the Northwest Highlands, the Great European Plain, the Central Highlands, and the Alpine System. The extreme northwestern region, the Northwest Highlands, extends through northwestern France, the northern British Isles, and Scandinavia. Parts of these highlands were once covered by huge glaciers, or sheets of ice, during the ice ages. These glaciers carved deep paths, or fiords, through the mountains on their way to the sea. In some places they carried away the soil. Therefore, much of this region is not good for agriculture. Where possible, people have used this land for grazing. Many of the people have turned to the sea for a living.

The Great European or Central Plain stretches from the Atlantic coast of France eastward to the Ural Mountains. It includes southern England and southern Sweden. In Russia, these plains extend from the Arctic south to the Caspian Sea. Near the Arctic the plain is called *tundra*—a cold, flat region where the soil is frozen much of the time and where only a few low plants will grow. Sections of this plain in western Europe and Ukraine are some of the world's richest farmlands. In the lowlands of this plain, people have had to build dikes and dams to prevent the area from being drowned by the sea.

South of the Great European Plain are the Central Highlands. This region begins at the Massif Central, a plateau in central France, and it stretches eastward to Russia. These highlands are very heavily forested. In all of these and other highland regions of Europe, there are many small plains and plateaus that are important agricultural areas.

The Alpine Mountain System covers much of southern Europe and is famous for its great beauty. The mountains extend from Spain eastward to the Caspian Sea. Its principal ranges are the Sierra Nevada, Pyrenees, Alps, Apennines, Carpathians, Balkans, and Caucasus. Mont Blanc, 15,771 feet (4,807 meters) above sea level, is the highest point in the Alps. Mt. Elbrus, in the Caucasus, is the highest point in Europe at 18,510 feet (5,642 meters) above sea level. Geographers who do not consider the Caucasus as part of Europe but as the southwestern boundary of Asia, do not consider Mt. Elbrus to be the highest point in Europe.

Generally Europe has a mild, temperate climate, and most of it receives adequate rainfall. In eastern and northern Europe and the central part of the Iberian Peninsula, there are greater extremes of temperature.

1. What four capital cities lie on the Danube River? They are the capitals of what countries?
2. What two countries lie partly in Europe and partly in Asia?
3. What do the capitals of Iceland, Norway, Sweden, Denmark, and Finland have in common?
4. What are the four natural land regions of Europe?

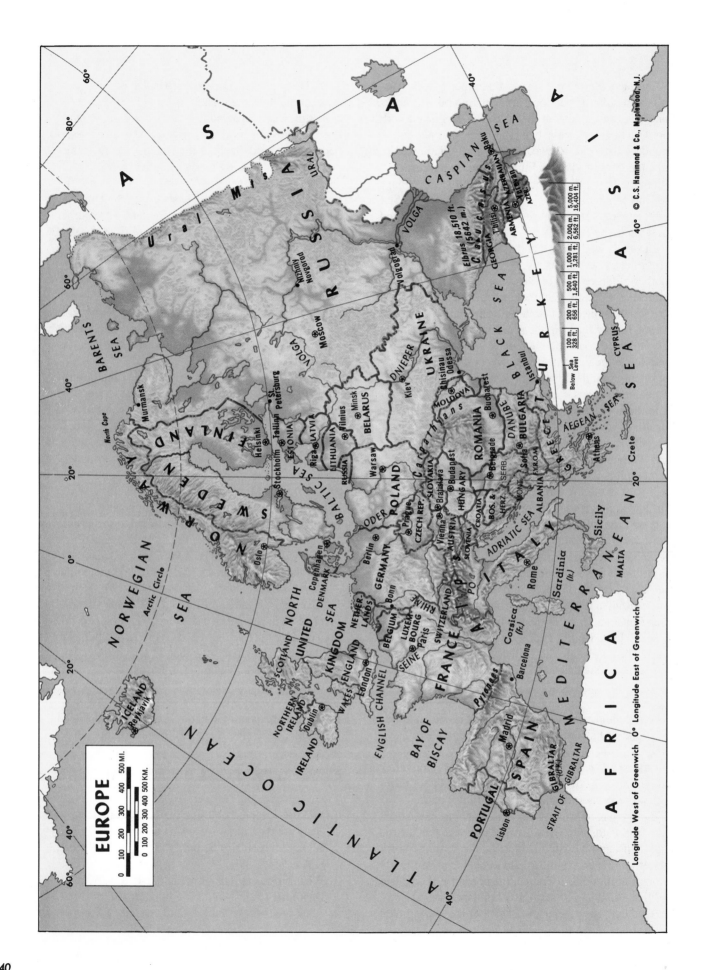

EUROPE

ASIA

RUSSIA

URAL Mts.

Ural Mts.

BARENTS SEA

CASPIAN SEA

VOLGA

Baku

AZERBAIJAN
Yerevan
ARMENIA
Tbilisi
GEORGIA
Caucasus
Elbrus 18,510 ft. (5,642 m.)

TURKEY

BLACK SEA

Nizhniy Novgorod

Volgograd

VOLGA

Moscow

DNIEPER

UKRAINE

Kiev

Chisinau
MOLDOVA

Odessa

Istanbul

CYPRUS

AEGEAN SEA

Crete

North Cape

Murmansk

St. Petersburg

Tallinn
ESTONIA
Riga
LATVIA
LITHUANIA
Vilnius

Minsk
BELARUS

Warsaw

Carpathians

Bucharest
ROMANIA
DANUBE
BULGARIA
Sofia
Belgrade
SERB.
F.Y.R.O.M.
ALBANIA

GREECE

Athens

NORWEGIAN SEA

Arctic Circle

Helsinki

FINLAND

Stockholm

BALTIC SEA

SWEDEN

NORWAY

Oslo

ODER

POLAND

Prague
CZECH REP.
SLOVAKIA
Bratislava
Vienna
AUSTRIA
HUNGARY
Budapest
SLOVENIA
CROATIA
BOS. & HERZ.
MONT.
ADRIATIC SEA

Berlin

GERMANY

Bonn

RHINE

Copenhagen
DENMARK

NORTH SEA

NETHER-LANDS

BELGIUM
LUXEM-BOURG

SWITZERLAND

ALPS

ITALY

Rome

Sardinia (It.)

Sicily

MALTA

MEDITERRANEAN SEA

ICELAND
Reykjavik

SCOTLAND

UNITED KINGDOM

NORTHERN IRELAND

IRELAND
Dublin

WALES
ENGLAND
London

ENGLISH CHANNEL

SEINE
Paris

FRANCE

Po R.

Corsica (Fr.)

Barcelona

BAY OF BISCAY

Pyrenees

SPAIN
Madrid

PORTUGAL
Lisbon

GIBRALTAR
GIBRALTAR (U.K.)
STRAIT OF GIBRALTAR

AFRICA

ATLANTIC OCEAN

Below Sea Level	Sea Level	100 m. 328 ft.	200 m. 656 ft.

500 m. 1,640 ft. | 1,000 m. 3,281 ft. | 2,000 m. 6,562 ft. | 5,000 m. 16,404 ft.

© C.S. Hammond & Co., Maplewood, N.J.

Longitude West of Greenwich 0° Longitude East of Greenwich

0 100 200 300 400 500 MI.
0 100 200 300 400 500 KM.

80° 60° 40° 20° 0° 20° 40° 60° 80° 40°

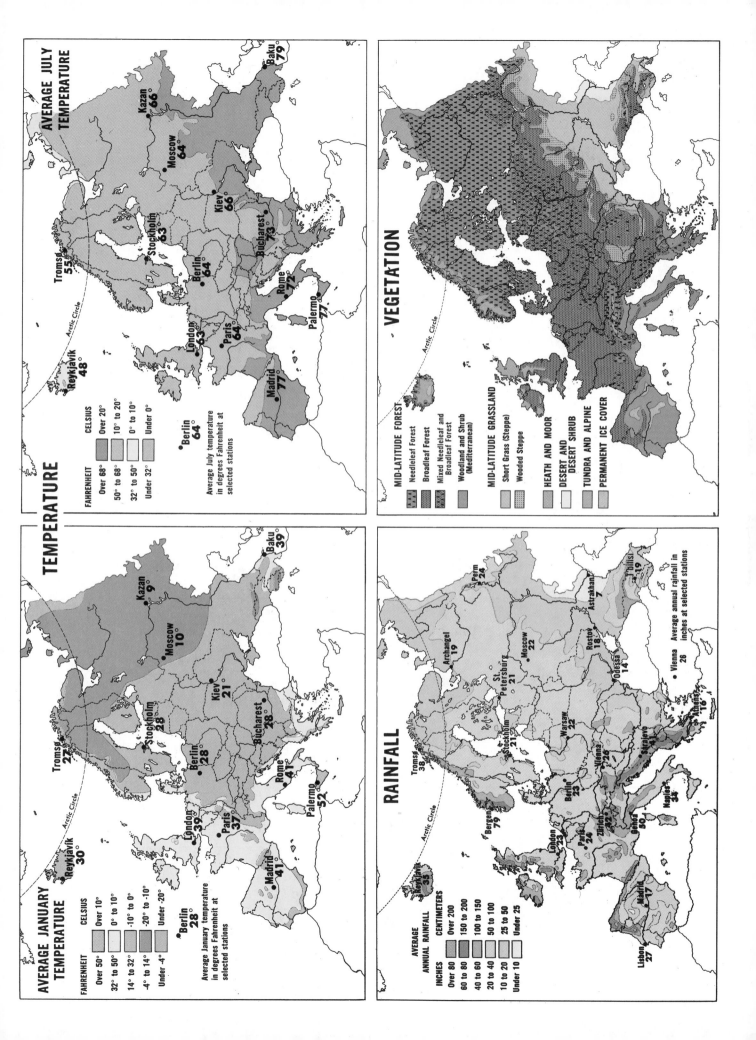

TEMPERATURE

AVERAGE JANUARY TEMPERATURE

FAHRENHEIT	CELSIUS
Over 50°	Over 10°
32° to 50°	0° to 10°
14° to 32°	-10° to 0°
-4° to 14°	-20° to -10°
Under -4°	Under -20°

• Berlin 28°

Average January temperature in degrees Fahrenheit at selected stations

Tromsø 27°
Reykjavik 30°
Kazan 9°
Moscow 10°
Baku 39°
Stockholm 28°
Kiev 21°
Bucharest 28°
Berlin 28°
London 39°
Paris 37°
Rome 41°
Palermo 52°
Madrid 41°

Arctic Circle

AVERAGE JULY TEMPERATURE

FAHRENHEIT	CELSIUS
Over 68°	Over 20°
50° to 68°	10° to 20°
32° to 50°	0° to 10°
Under 32°	Under 0°

• Berlin 64°

Average July temperature in degrees Fahrenheit at selected stations

Baku 79°
Kazan 66°
Moscow 64°
Tromsø 55°
Stockholm 63°
Kiev 66°
Bucharest 73°
Berlin 64°
Reykjavik 48°
London 63°
Paris 64°
Rome 72°
Palermo 77°
Madrid 77°

Arctic Circle

VEGETATION

MID-LATITUDE FOREST
- Needleleaf Forest
- Broadleaf Forest
- Mixed Needleleaf and Broadleaf Forest
- Woodland and Shrub (Mediterranean)

MID-LATITUDE GRASSLAND
- Short Grass (Steppe)
- Wooded Steppe

- HEATH AND MOOR
- DESERT AND DESERT SHRUB
- TUNDRA AND ALPINE
- PERMANENT ICE COVER

Arctic Circle

RAINFALL

AVERAGE ANNUAL RAINFALL	
INCHES	CENTIMETERS
Over 80	Over 200
60 to 80	150 to 200
40 to 60	100 to 150
20 to 40	50 to 100
10 to 20	25 to 50
Under 10	Under 25

• Vienna 26

Average annual rainfall in inches at selected stations

Tromsø 38
Perm 24
Archangel 19
St. Petersburg 21
Moscow 22
Astrakhan 7
Rostov 18
Odessa 14
Tbilisi 19
Stockholm 21
Warsaw 22
Bergen 79
Vienna 26
Berlin 23
Sarajevo
London 23
Paris 24
Zürich 43
Genoa 50
Athens 16
Naples 34
Reykjavik 35
Lisbon 27
Madrid 17

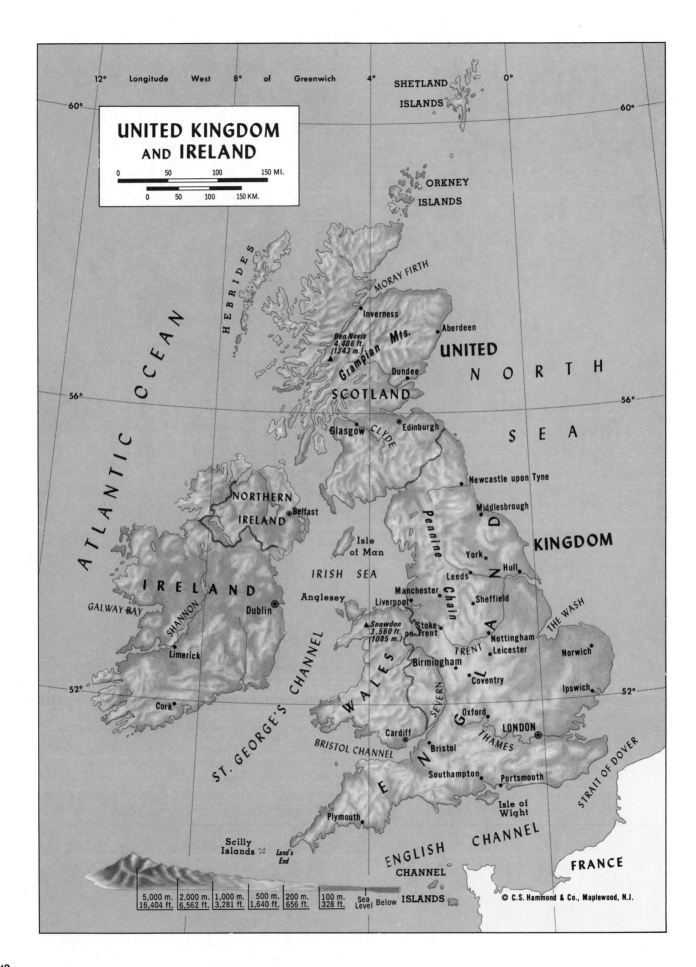

UNITED KINGDOM
AND IRELAND

0   50   100   150 MI.

0   50   100   150 KM.

12° Longitude West 8° of Greenwich 4° 0°

60°   60°

SHETLAND
ISLANDS

ORKNEY
ISLANDS

HEBRIDES

ATLANTIC OCEAN

MORAY FIRTH

Inverness

Ben Nevis
4,406 ft.
(1343 m.)

Grampian Mts.

Aberdeen

UNITED

Dundee

SCOTLAND

N O R T H

56°   56°

Glasgow   CLYDE   Edinburgh

S E A

Newcastle upon Tyne

Middlesbrough

NORTHERN
IRELAND   Belfast

KINGDOM

Isle
of Man

Pennine

York

Hull

IRELAND

Irish Sea

Leeds

Chain

Sheffield

L A N D

GALWAY BAY

SHANNON

Dublin

Anglesey

Manchester
Liverpool

Stoke-
on-Trent

ST. GEORGE'S CHANNEL

Snowdon
3,560 ft.
(1085 m.)

TRENT

Nottingham
Leicester

THE WASH

Norwich

Limerick

WALES

Birmingham

Coventry

E N G L A N D

SEVERN

Ipswich

52°   52°

Cork

Oxford

Cardiff

THAMES

LONDON

Bristol

BRISTOL CHANNEL

Southampton   Portsmouth

STRAIT OF DOVER

Plymouth

Isle of
Wight

Scilly
Islands

Land's
End

ENGLISH   CHANNEL

CHANNEL
ISLANDS

FRANCE

© C.S. Hammond & Co., Maplewood, N.J.

5,000 m.   2,000 m.   1,000 m.   500 m.   200 m.   100 m.   Sea   Below
16,404 ft.   6,562 ft.   3,281 ft.   1,640 ft.   656 ft.   328 ft.   Level

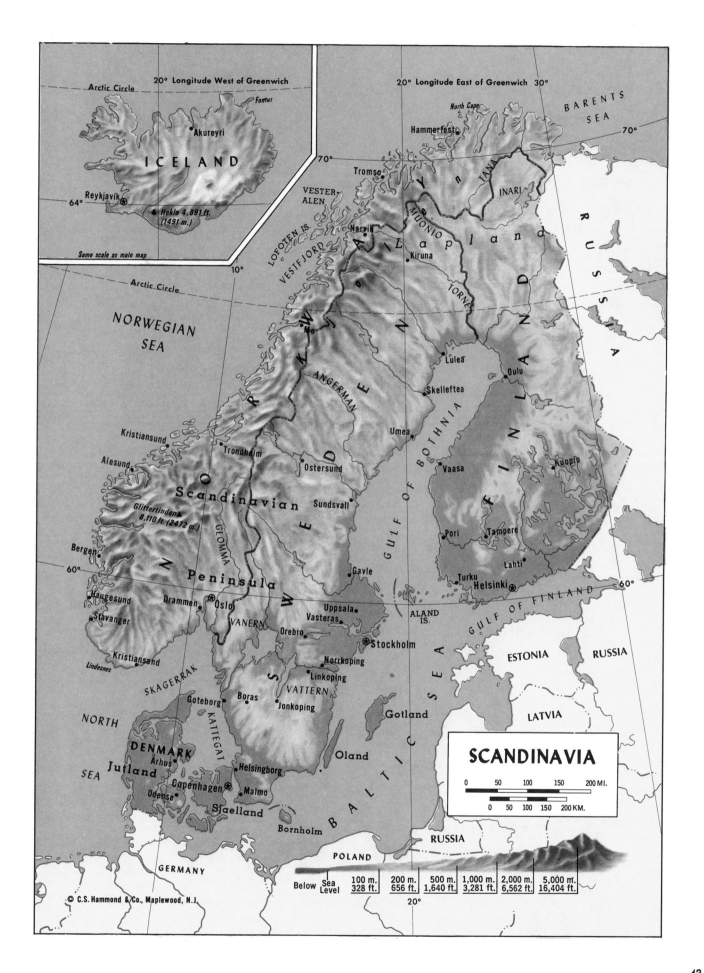

20° Longitude West of Greenwich

Arctic Circle

Fontur

Akureyri

ICELAND

64°

Reykjavik ⊕

▲ Hekla 4,891 ft.
(1491 m.)

Same scale as main map

10°

20° Longitude East of Greenwich   30°

BARENTS
SEA

North Cape

Hammerfest

70°

70°

Tromsø

VESTER-
ALEN

TANA

INARI

RUSSIA

Narvik

MUONIO

Kiruna

L a p l a n d

LOFOTEN IS.

VESTFJORD

TORNE

Arctic Circle

NORWEGIAN
SEA

Me

Lulea

Oulu

ANGERMAN

Skelleftea

Kristiansund

Trondheim

Umea

GULF OF BOTHNIA

F I N L A N D

Vaasa

Kuopio

Alesund

Ostersund

Scandinavian

Sundsvall

Pori

Tampere

Glittertinden▲
8,110 ft. (2472 m.)

GLOMMA

Lahti

Bergen

60°

Peninsula

Gavle

Turku

Helsinki ⊕

60°

Haugesund

Drammen

Oslo

Uppsala

ALAND
IS.

GULF OF FINLAND

Stavanger

VANERN

Vasteras

Orebro

Stockholm ⊕

ESTONIA

RUSSIA

Kristiansand

Norrkoping

BALTIC SEA

Lindesnes

SKAGERRAK

Linkoping

LATVIA

Boras

VATTERN

Goteborg

Gotland

NORTH

KATTEGAT

Jonkoping

Oland

DENMARK

Arhus

Helsingborg

SEA

Jutland

Copenhagen ⊕

Malmo

Odense

Sjaelland

Bornholm

GERMANY

POLAND

RUSSIA

SCANDINAVIA

0   50   100   150   200 MI.

0   50   100   150   200 KM.

Below   Sea
Level

100 m.
328 ft.

200 m.
656 ft.

500 m.
1,640 ft.

1,000 m.
3,281 ft.

2,000 m.
6,562 ft.

5,000 m.
16,404 ft.

20°

© C.S. Hammond & Co., Maplewood, N.J.

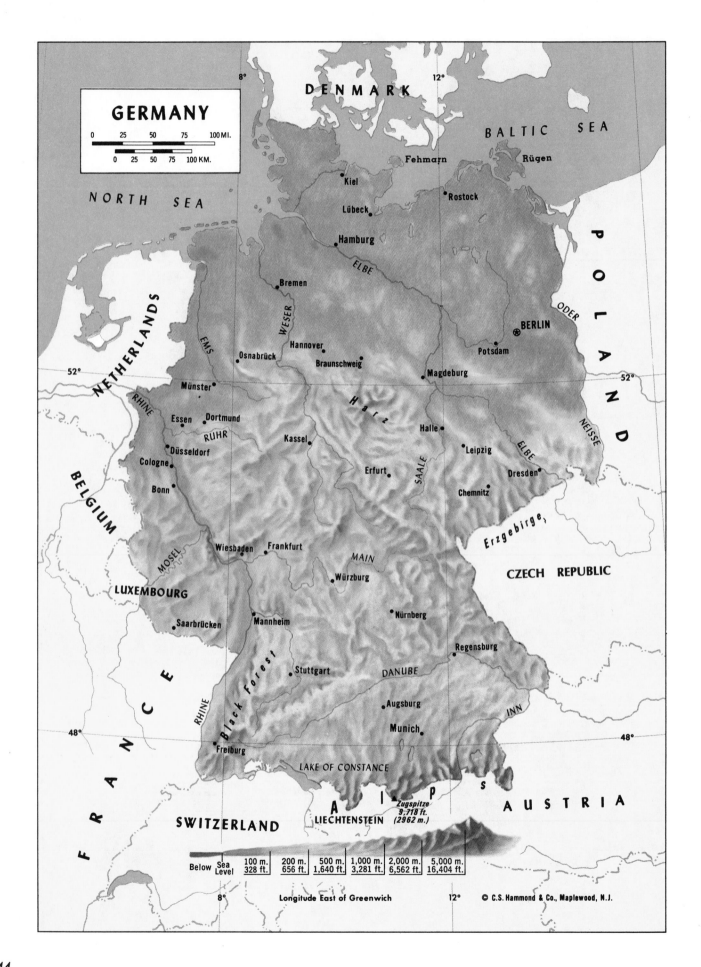

GERMANY

DENMARK

BALTIC SEA

NORTH SEA

POLAND

NETHERLANDS

BELGIUM

LUXEMBOURG

FRANCE

SWITZERLAND

LIECHTENSTEIN

AUSTRIA

CZECH REPUBLIC

Fehmarn
Rügen
Kiel
Rostock
Lübeck
Hamburg
Bremen
Osnabrück
Hannover
Braunschweig
Münster
Magdeburg
BERLIN
Potsdam
Essen
Dortmund
Kassel
Halle
Leipzig
Düsseldorf
Dresden
Cologne
Erfurt
Chemnitz
Bonn
Wiesbaden
Frankfurt
Würzburg
Saarbrücken
Mannheim
Nürnberg
Regensburg
Stuttgart
DANUBE
Augsburg
Munich
Freiburg

ELBE
WESER
EMS
RHINE
RUHR
Harz
SAALE
ODER
NEISSE
ELBE
Erzgebirge
MAIN
MOSEL
RHINE
Black Forest
INN

LAKE OF CONSTANCE

ALPS

▲ Zugspitze
9,718 ft.
(2962 m.)

Longitude East of Greenwich

© C.S. Hammond & Co., Maplewood, N.J.

| Below Sea Level | 100 m. 328 ft. | 200 m. 656 ft. | 500 m. 1,640 ft. | 1,000 m. 3,281 ft. | 2,000 m. 6,562 ft. | 5,000 m. 16,404 ft. |

Scale: 0 25 50 75 100 MI.
0 25 50 75 100 KM.

8°   12°   52°   48°

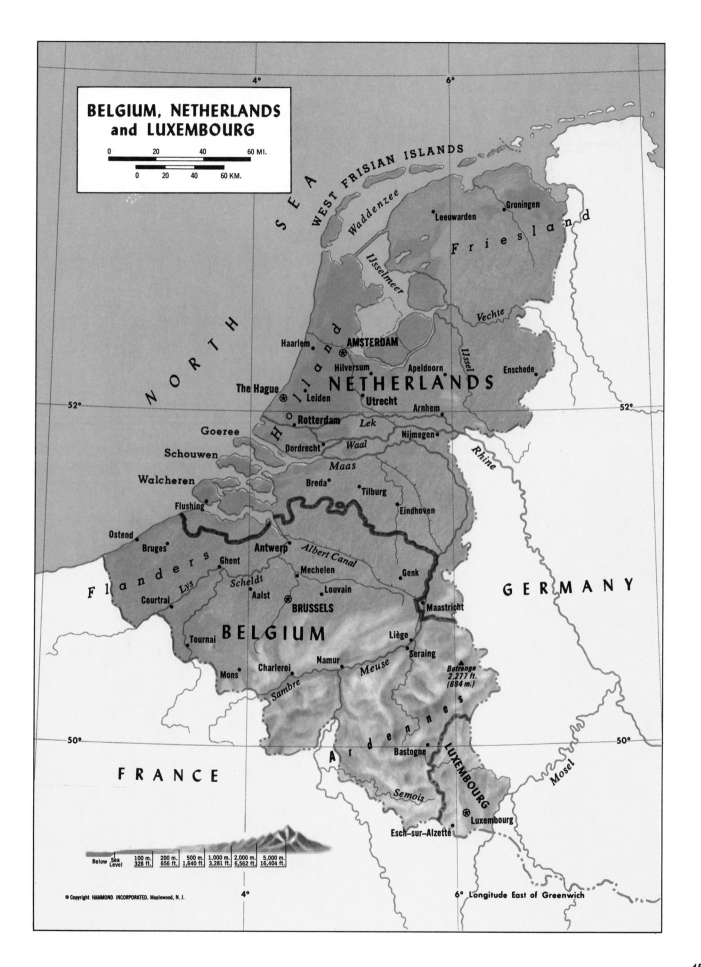

BELGIUM, NETHERLANDS and LUXEMBOURG

0 20 40 60 MI.

0 20 40 60 KM.

NORTH SEA

WEST FRISIAN ISLANDS

Waddenzee

IJsselmeer

Friesland

• Leeuwarden

• Groningen

Vechte

Haarlem •

AMSTERDAM ⊛

H o l l a n d

Hilversum •

• Apeldoorn

IJssel

Enschede •

The Hague ⊛

• Leiden

NETHERLANDS

Utrecht •

Arnhem •

52°

52°

• Rotterdam

Lek

Nijmegen •

Goeree

Dordrecht •

Waal

Schouwen

Maas

Rhine

Walcheren

Breda •

Tilburg •

Flushing •

Eindhoven •

Ostend •

Bruges •

F l a n d e r s

Ghent •

Antwerp •

Albert Canal

Genk •

Lys

Scheldt

Mechelen •

Courtrai •

Aalst •

BRUSSELS ⊛

• Louvain

Maastricht •

GERMANY

Tournai •

BELGIUM

Namur •

Liège •

Seraing •

Mons •

Charleroi •

Meuse

Botrange

2,277 ft.

(694 m.)

Sambre

A r d e n n e s

50°

50°

Bastogne •

LUXEMBOURG

FRANCE

Semois

Mosel

⊛ Luxembourg

Esch–sur–Alzette •

Below Sea Level | 100 m. 328 ft. | 200 m. 656 ft. | 500 m. 1,640 ft. | 1,000 m. 3,281 ft. | 2,000 m. 6,562 ft. | 5,000 m. 16,404 ft.

4°

6° Longitude East of Greenwich

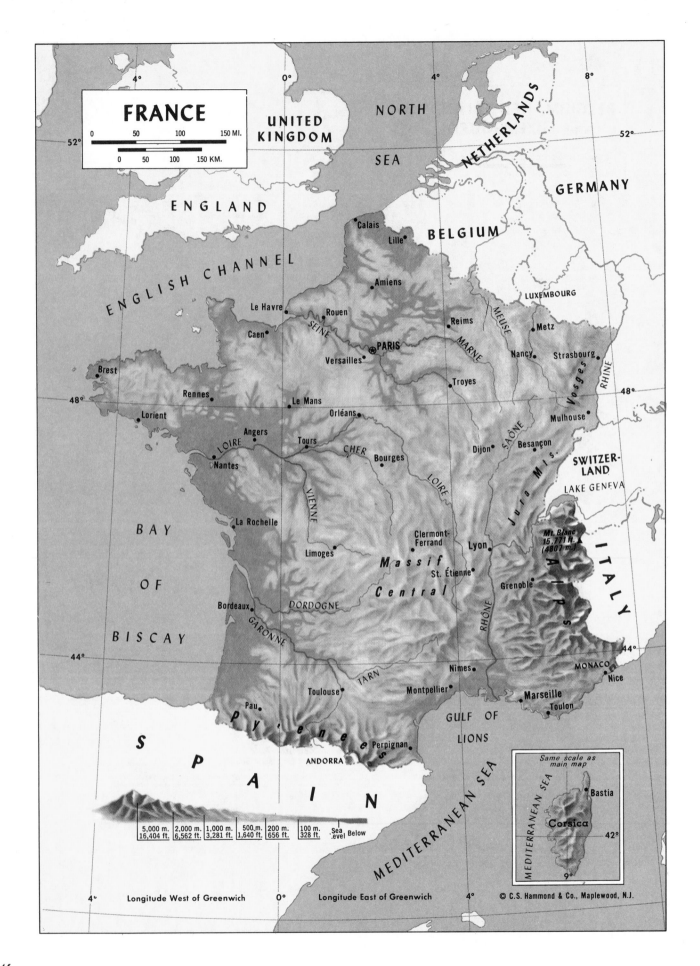

FRANCE

0   50   100   150 MI.

0   50   100   150 KM.

UNITED
KINGDOM

NORTH
SEA

NETHERLANDS

GERMANY

52°

52°

ENGLAND

ENGLISH CHANNEL

Calais
Lille

BELGIUM

Amiens

LUXEMBOURG

Le Havre
Rouen
Reims
Metz

Caen
SEINE
Nancy
Strasbourg

MARNE
MEUSE

PARIS
Versailles
Troyes

Vosges
RHINE

Brest

48°
48°

Rennes
Le Mans
Orléans
SAÔNE
Besançon
Mulhouse

Lorient
Dijon
Jura Mts.
SWITZERLAND

Angers
Tours
CHER
Bourges
LAKE GENEVA

LOIRE
Nantes
LOIRE

VIENNE
Mt. Blanc
15,771 ft.
(4807 m.)

BAY
La Rochelle
Clermont-
Ferrand
Lyon
ITALY

OF
Limoges
Massif
St. Étienne
Grenoble
A
L
P
S

BISCAY
DORDOGNE
Central
RHÔNE

Bordeaux
GARONNE
MONACO
Nice

44°
TARN
Nîmes
44°

Toulouse
Montpellier
Marseille
Toulon

Pau
Pyrénées
Perpignan
GULF OF
LIONS

S   P   A   I   N
ANDORRA

5,000 m.   2,000 m.   1,000 m.   500 m.   200 m.   100 m.   Sea   Below
16,404 ft.   6,562 ft.   3,281 ft.   1,640 ft.   656 ft.   328 ft.   level

Same scale as
main map

MEDITERRANEAN SEA
Bastia

MEDITERRANEAN SEA
Corsica
42°

9°

4°   Longitude West of Greenwich   0°   Longitude East of Greenwich   4°   © C.S. Hammond & Co., Maplewood, N.J.

46

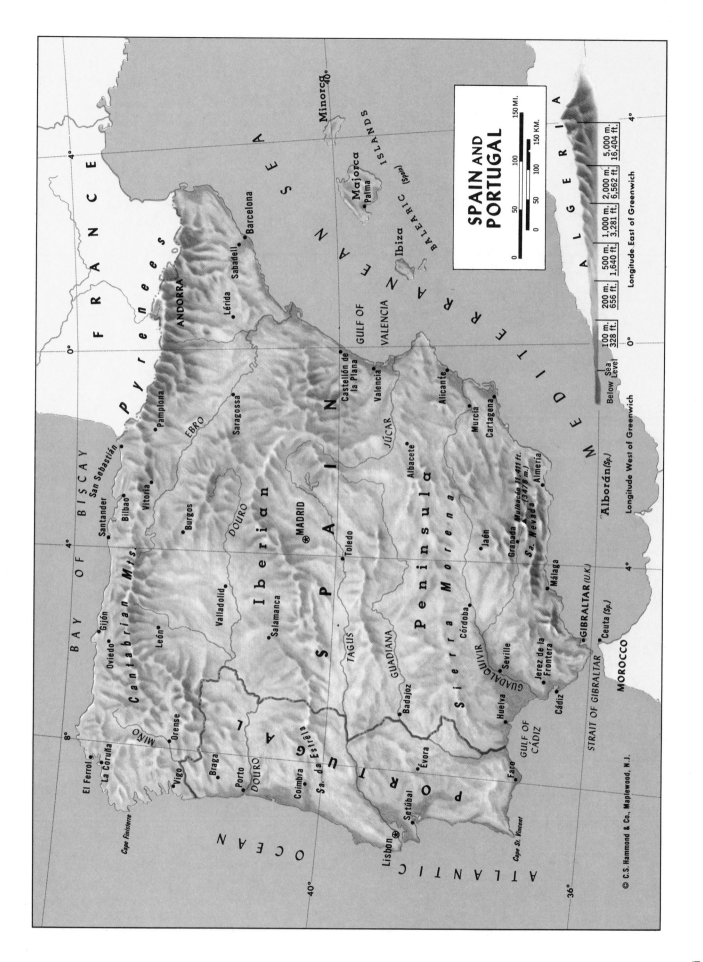

SPAIN AND
PORTUGAL

150 MI.

| 100 | 150 KM. |

50	100
0	50
0	

Longitude East of Greenwich

5,000 m.	16,404 ft.
2,000 m.	6,562 ft.
1,000 m.	3,281 ft.
500 m.	1,640 ft.
200 m.	656 ft.
100 m.	328 ft.
Sea Level	
Below Sea Level	

Longitude West of Greenwich

FRANCE

Pyrenees

BAY OF BISCAY

San Sebastián
Santander
Bilbao
Vitoria
Burgos

Cantabrian Mts.

Gijón
Oviedo
León

Orense

MIÑO

El Ferrol
La Coruña
Vigo
Braga
Porto

Cape Finisterre

ATLANTIC OCEAN

ANDORRA
Pamplona
EBRO
Saragossa

Lérida
Sabadell
Barcelona

SPAIN

Iberian

Valladolid
Salamanca

MADRID

Toledo
TAGUS

DOURO

GUADIANA
Badajoz

Évora

PORTUGAL

Sa. da Estrêla
Coimbra
DOURO

Setúbal
Lisbon

Faro

Cape St. Vincent

GULF OF CÁDIZ

Huelva
Cádiz
Jerez de la Frontera
Seville

GUADALQUIVIR

Córdoba

Sierra Morena

Peninsula

Jaén

Granada
Sa. Nevada
Mulhacén 11,411 ft. (3,478 m.)
Almería

Málaga

Castellón de la Plana
Valencia
JÚCAR
Albacete

Alicante
Murcia
Cartagena

GULF OF VALENCIA

VALENCIA

MEDITERRANEAN SEA

Ibiza
BALEARIC (Sp.)

Majorca
Palma

Minorca

BALEARIC ISLANDS

ALGERIA

Alborán (Sp.)

GIBRALTAR (U.K.)
Ceuta (Sp.)
STRAIT OF GIBRALTAR
MOROCCO

FRANCE

© C.S. Hammond & Co., Maplewood, N.J.

47

GERMANY

AUSTRIA

HUNGARY

LIECHTENSTEIN

SWITZERLAND

SLOVENIA

CROATIA

Mte. Rosa
15,203 ft.
(4634 m.)

Trento

Trieste

BOSNIA
&
HERZEGOVINA

Brescia

Padua

Milan

Verona

Venice

Turin

ADIGE

PO

PO

Parma

Ferrara

Genoa

Bologna

ADRIATIC

Florence

SAN
MARINO

Ancona

Leghorn

ARNO

LIGURIAN
SEA

Siena

Elba

Pescara

Viterbo

TIBER

SEA

VATICAN CITY

ROME

CORSICA
(Fr.)

Latina

Foggia

Bari

TYRRHENIAN

Vesuvius
4,190 ft.
(1277 m.)

Naples

Taranto

Salerno

Sardinia

GULF OF
TARANTO

SEA

Cagliari

IONIAN

MEDITERRANEAN

Messina

Palermo

Reggio di Calabria

SEA

Etna 11,053 ft.
(3369 m.)

Sicily

Catania

SEA

Pantelleria

C. Passero

ITALY

0   50   100   150 MI.

0   50   100   150 KM.

MALTA

Longitude East of Greenwich

© C.S. Hammond & Co., Maplewood, N.J.

5,000 m. | 2,000 m. | 1,000 m. | 500 m. | 200 m. | 100 m. | Sea | Below
16,404 ft. | 6,562 ft. | 3,281 ft. | 1,640 ft. | 656 ft. | 328 ft. | Level |

FRANCE

A L P S

A P E N N I N E S

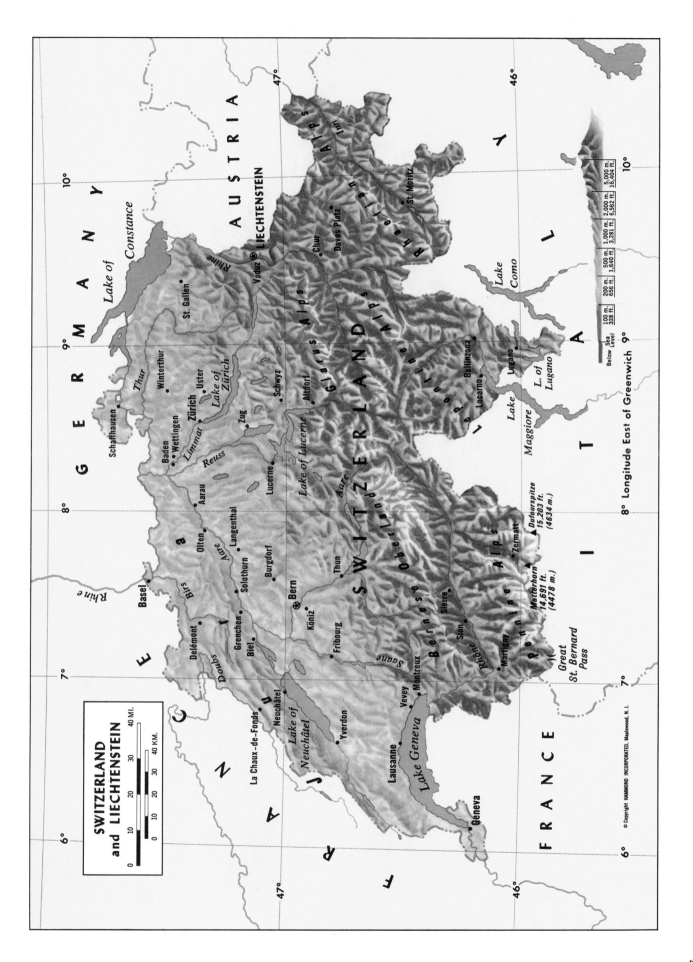

SWITZERLAND and LIECHTENSTEIN

0 10 20 30 40 MI.

0 10 20 30 40 KM.

G E R M A N Y

A U S T R I A

LIECHTENSTEIN
Vaduz

Lake of Constance

F R A N C E

I T A L Y

S W I T Z E R L A N D

Rhine
Schaffhausen
St. Gallen
Winterthur
Thur
Uster
Zürich
Lake of Zürich
Baden
Wettingen
Zug
Schwyz
Limmat
Reuss
Altdorf
Lucerne
Lake of Lucerne
Aarau
Olten
Langenthal
Langnau
Burgdorf
Solothurn
Aare
Basel
Birs
Delémont
Grenchen
Biel
Bern
Köniz
Fribourg
Thun
Aare
Saane
Rhine
Doubs
La Chaux-de-Fonds
Neuchâtel
Lake of Neuchâtel
Yverdon
Lausanne
Lake Geneva
Vevey
Montreux
Geneva
Sierre
Sion
Martigny
Rhône
Great St. Bernard Pass
Zermatt
Matterhorn 14,691 ft. (4478 m.)
Dufourspitze 15,203 ft. (4634 m.)
Chur
Davos Platz
St. Moritz
Bellinzona
Locarno
Lugano
L. of Lugano
Lake Maggiore
Lake Como
Rheinian Alps
Glarus Alps
Inn
Rhône
Oberland Alps
Bernese Alps
Pennine Alps

J U R A

A L P S

Sea Level Below | 100 m. 328 ft. | 200 m. 656 ft. | 500 m. 1,640 ft. | 1,000 m. 3,281 ft. | 2,000 m. 6,562 ft. | 5,000 m. 16,404 ft.

8° Longitude East of Greenwich 9°

© Copyright HAMMOND INCORPORATED. Maplewood, N.J.

47° 10° 46°

49

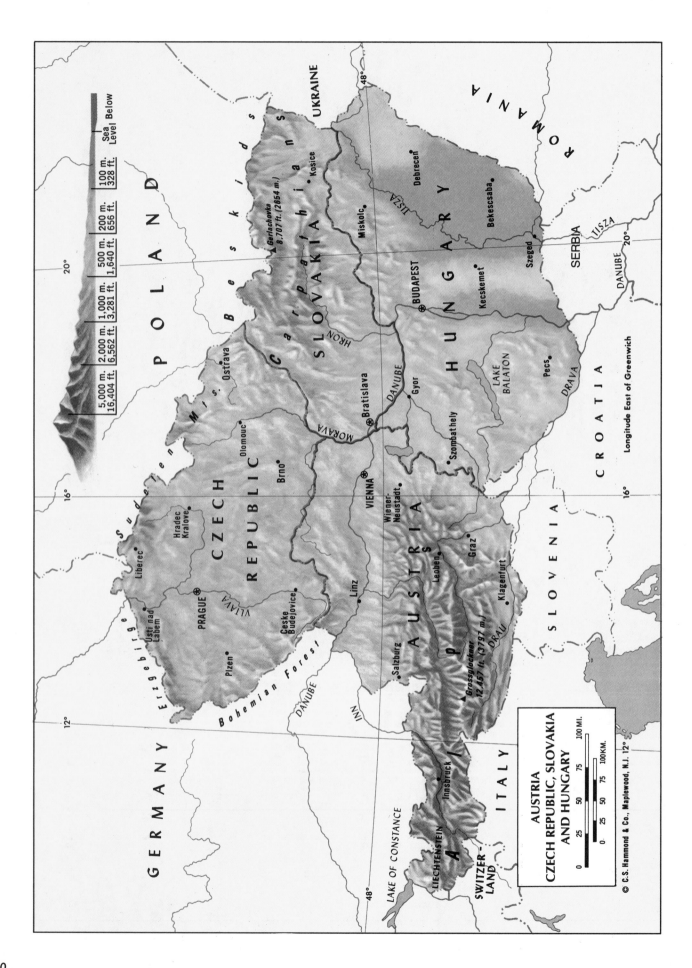

POLAND

5,000 m. | 2,000 m. | 1,000 m. | 500 m. | 200 m. | 100 m.
16,404 ft. | 6,562 ft. | 3,281 ft. | 1,640 ft. | 656 ft. | 328 ft.

Sea
Level Below

UKRAINE

ROMANIA

Sudeten Mts.

Beskids

Carpathians

Ostrava

Kosice

▲ Gerlachovka (2654 m.)
8,707 ft.

Debrecen

Miskolc

Bekessaba

TISZA

SLOVAKIA

Olomouc

Brno

CZECH

REPUBLIC

HRON

BUDAPEST ⊕

Szeged

SERBIA

TISZA

DANUBE

GERMANY

Erzgebirge

Liberec

Hradec
Kralove

Bratislava ⊕

MORAVA

DANUBE

Gyor

HUNGARY

Kecskemet

Pecs

DRAVA

 Usti nad
Labem

PRAGUE ⊕

VLTAVA

Ceske
Budejovice

Linz

VIENNA ⊕

Wiener-
Neustadt

Szombathely

LAKE
BALATON

CROATIA

Pilzen

Bohemian Forest

DANUBE

INN

AUSTRIA

S

Leoben

Graz

Klagenfurt

DRAU

SLOVENIA

Salzburg

A
L
P
S

▲ Grossglockner
12,457 ft. (3797 m.)

Innsbruck

ITALY

LIECHTENSTEIN

A

LAKE OF CONSTANCE

SWITZER-
LAND

Longitude East of Greenwich

AUSTRIA
CZECH REPUBLIC, SLOVAKIA
AND HUNGARY

0   25   50   75   100 MI.

0   25   50   75   100 KM.

© C.S. Hammond & Co., Maplewood, N.J. 12°

50

POLAND

CZECH REP.

UKRAINE

SLOVAKIA

AUSTRIA

HUNGARY

TISZA

Oradea

CARPATHIANS

Cluj-Napoca

Iasi   MOLDOVA

PRUT

Ljubljana

SLOVENIA

DRAVA

Zagreb

Subotica

Arad

MURES

ROMANIA

CROATIA

DANUBE

TISZA

Timisoara

Rijeka

SAVA

Novi Sad

Brasov

Alps

Galati

Dinaric

Belgrade

Transylvanian

Ploiesti

BOSNIA &

MORAVA

Bucharest

HERZEGOVINA

SERBIA

Craiova

OLT

Constanta

Sarajevo

DANUBE

Split

Ruse

Balkan

Nis

Pleven

Varna

Alps

MONT.

Sofia

Mts.

BLACK

Podgorica

BULGARIA

SEA

Rhodope

Plovdiv

Burgas

DRIN

Shkoder

Skopje

VARDAR

MARITSA

ADRIATIC

FORMER

YUGO.

Mts.

Tirane

REP. OF

MACEDONIA

SEA

Kavalla

ITALY

ALBANIA

Salonika

TURKEY

Vlore

Pindus

Olympus

9,570 ft.

(2917 m.)

Larisa

AEGEAN

40°

40°

Corfu

GREECE

Lesbos

IONIAN

Mts.

Euboea

Chios

SEA

Sicily

Patras

Piraeus

Athens

SEA

Peloponnesos

CYCLADES

Rhodes

THE BALKANS

0   50   100   150   200 MI.

0   50   100   150   200 KM.

Candia

Crete

MEDITERRANEAN   SEA

20°   Longitude East of Greenwich

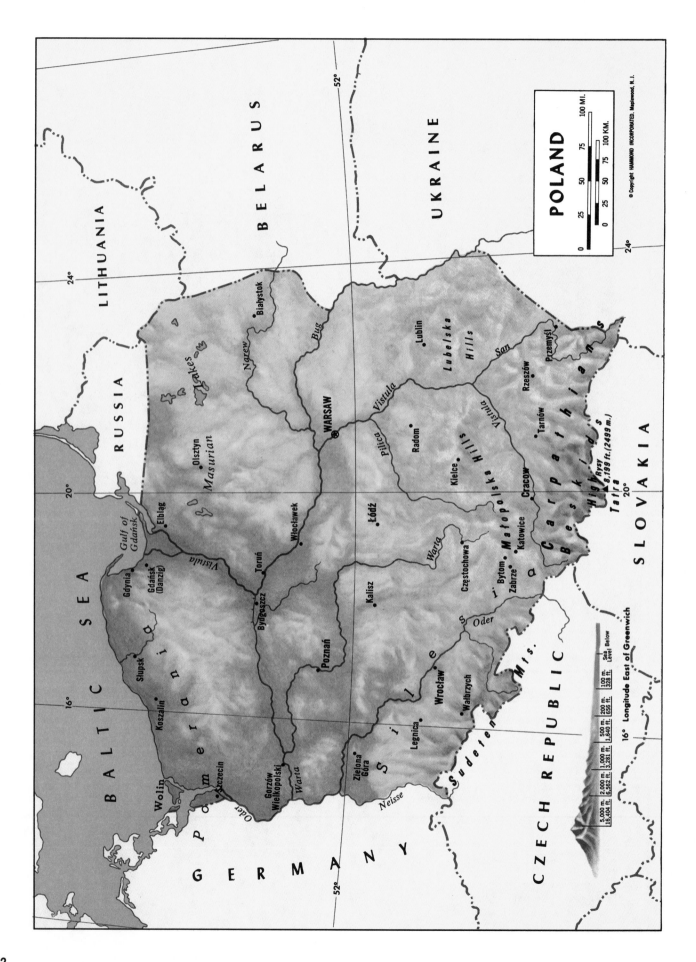

POLAND

© Copyright: HAMMOND INCORPORATED. Maplewood, N.J.

100 MI.
100 KM.
75
50
25
0

BALTIC SEA

LITHUANIA

RUSSIA

BELARUS

UKRAINE

GERMANY

CZECH REPUBLIC

SLOVAKIA

Wolin
Szczecin
Koszalin
Słupsk
Gdynia
Gdańsk (Danzig)
Elbląg
Gulf of Gdańsk
Olsztyn
Masurian Lakes
Białystok
Narew
Bug
Lublin
Lubelska Hills
San
Przemyśl
Rzeszów
Tarnów
WARSAW
Vistula
Pilica
Radom
Kielce
Włocławek
Toruń
Bydgoszcz
Łódź
Vistula
Kalisz
Częstochowa
Warta
Oder
Poznań
Gorzów Wielkopolski
Warta
Zielona Góra
Neisse
Legnica
Wrocław
Wałbrzych
Sudeten Mts.
Bytom
Zabrze
Katowice
Cracow
Małopolska Hills
High Tatra
Rysy 8,199 ft. (2499 m.)
Carpathians
Beskids
Vistula
Silesia
Pomerania

5,000 m. 2,000 m. 1,000 m. 500 m. 200 m. 100 m. Sea
16,404 ft. 6,562 ft. 3,281 ft. 1,640 ft. 656 ft. 328 ft. Level Below

16° Longitude East of Greenwich

24°
20°
16°
52°

52

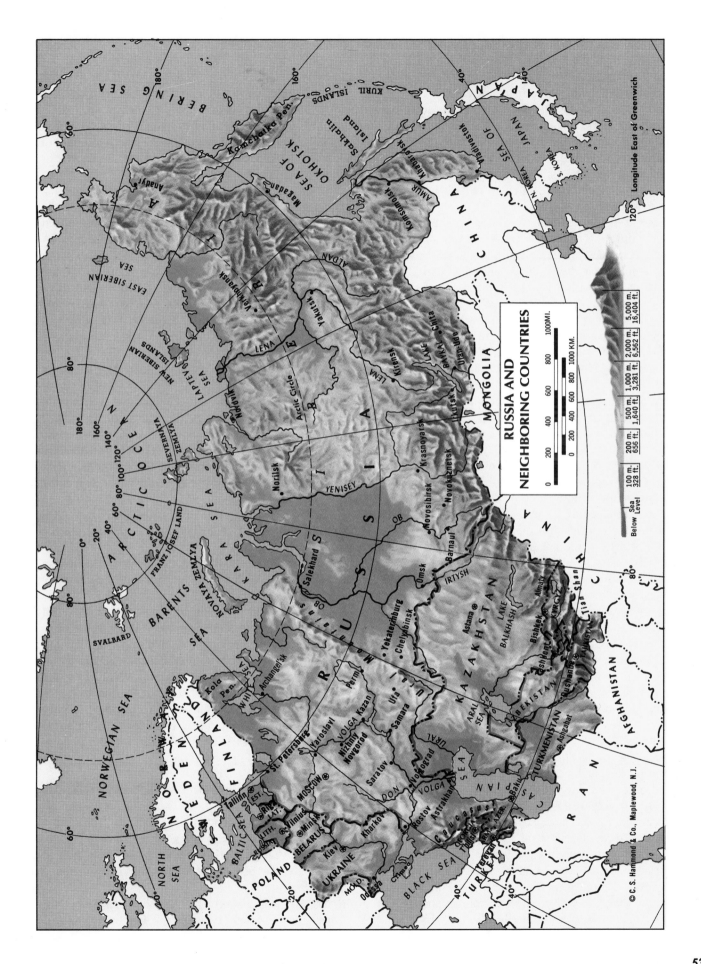

RUSSIA AND
NEIGHBORING COUNTRIES

Below Sea Level	100 m. 328 ft.	200 m. 656 ft.	500 m. 1,640 ft.	1,000 m. 3,281 ft.	2,000 m. 6,562 ft.	5,000 m. 16,404 ft.

0   200   400   600   800   1000MI.
0   200   400   600   800   1000 KM.

Longitude East of Greenwich

© C. S. Hammond & Co., Maplewood, N.J.

BERING SEA

Kamchatka Pen.

KURIL ISLANDS

Sakhalin Island

SEA OF OKHOTSK

Anadyr

Magadan

SEA OF JAPAN

JAPAN

Vladivostok

NORTH KOREA

S. KOREA

CHINA

EAST SIBERIAN SEA

NEW SIBERIAN ISLANDS

LAPTEV SEA

Verkhoyansk

ALDAN

Khabarovsk

AMUR

Komsomolsk

Yakutsk

LENA

SEVERNAYA ZEMLYA

KARA SEA

Arctic Circle

Nordvik

LENA

Kirensk

LAKE BAIKAL

Chita

Ulan-Ude

MONGOLIA

ARCTIC OCEAN

FRANZ JOSEF LAND

Norilsk

YENISEY

Irkutsk

Krasnoyarsk

BARENTS SEA

NOVAYA ZEMLYA

SVALBARD

Salekhard

OB

Novosibirsk

Novokuznetsk

Barnaul

OB

Omsk

IRTYSH

LAKE BALKHASH

Almaty

Tian Shan

KYRGYZSTAN

Bishkek

Astana

KAZAKHSTAN

CHINA

NORWEGIAN SEA

WHITE SEA

Kola Pen.

Archangel'sk

Perm'

Yekaterinburg

Chelyabinsk

Ufa

URAL

Tashkent

UZBEKISTAN

Dushanbe

TAJIKISTAN

AFGHANISTAN

NORTH SEA

FINLAND

SWEDEN

St. Petersburg

Yaroslavl

VOLGA

Kazan

Nizhniy Novgorod

Samara

Saratov

ARAL SEA

TURKMENISTAN

Ashgabat

IRAN

Tallinn

EST.

Riga

LAT.

Vilnius

LITH.

Minsk

BELARUS

MOSCOW

DON

Volgograd

VOLGA

Astrakhan

CASPIAN SEA

Baku

AZER.

Caucasus

BALTIC SEA

RUSSIA

POLAND

Kiev

UKRAINE

Kharkov

Rostov

Odessa

MOLD.

BLACK SEA

Tbilisi

GEORGIA

ARM.

Yerevan

TURKEY

53

ASIA

Asia is the largest continent on earth. It extends almost halfway around the world and covers about one-third of the world's land area. It also has more people than any other continent. Over two billion people live here, which is about 60 percent of the world's population. Asia has more kinds of people and cultures than any other continent. In every way, it is the most varied of continents.

Look at the rainfall map of Asia and find the areas of heavy rainfall. These areas are the continent's most heavily populated places. You may wonder why, with so much land, people crowd into such a small part of Asia. Part of the answer lies in the continent's great size and the way the mountains extend across it.

If you look north of Pakistan, you will see mountains where Afghanistan, Tajikistan, China, and India meet. These mountains are the Pamir, and they form a knot of mountains which are sometimes called the "roof of the world." From this center, mountains spiral out in different directions, like the spokes of a wheel. They run westward into southern Europe. They stretch southeastward from the Pamir to form the highest mountains in the world, the Himalayas. The Himalayas' highest point, and the highest point on earth, is Mount Everest on the Nepal-China border. The mountains continue south in long lines of deep, forested ravines and continue as a string of islands offshore. The Himalayas and other mountains block the winds that blow north from the oceans and prevent these winds from reaching farther inland. The mountains also stop the cold winds in the north from reaching India. Because of these conditions the center of Asia is very dry and southern Asia is very wet.

From the Pamir knot, mountains run northeastward across Asia. Between the ranges are high plateaus and basins. North of the Himalayas is Tibet, the highest plateau in the world. It can support only a few people. These high, flat areas are not only cold and dry, they are among the most isolated places on earth. To the north of Tibet, between the Tian Shan, Kunlun, and other mountains, you will see lower areas, or basins. They are deserts. The dry land extends northeast through southern Mongolia. The Gobi, one of the world's great deserts, is found here. The few people who have settled in these areas live mostly on oases.

Dry mountainous lands continue southwestward from the Pamir through Pakistan and Afghanistan to merge with the dry plateaus of Iran, Turkey, and the Arabian peninsula. Almost all of southwestern Asia up to about 50° latitude is dry except for part of the land between the Tigris and Euphrates rivers. This region has some of the world's largest petroleum deposits.

North of this area the land becomes lower. It is mostly steppes—areas of short grass, which are mainly used for grazing. The steppes extend eastward across northern Mongolia, arc southward through northern China, and turn west through part of the Huang He, or Yellow River, valley.

All of Asia north of the mountains is a continuation of the Great European Plain, and it sinks slowly to the Arctic Ocean. The northernmost area is *tundra*—frozen flatland on which only a few low plants will grow. A zone of pine forests and swamps, called *taiga*, is between the tundra and steppes. Other plains of Asia are found in northern India and eastern China. These plains and the valleys of Southeast Asia are the major agricultural regions of Asia. Most of Asia is rich in mineral resources, but its nations are less industrialized than those in Europe and North America.

Most of the great rivers of Asia begin in the mountains and flow over cliffs and rocks and lowlands to empty sluggishly into the sea. Most of Asia's great civilizations were built along the valleys of the Yellow River, Yangtze, Brahmaputra-Ganges, Indus, Mekong, Irrawaddy, and Salween rivers. Many of these rivers carry soil, which they deposit at their mouths. Also, many of them regularly overflow their banks, leaving behind fresh layers of soil. The plains around these rivers are among the most fertile on earth. Unfortunately, this flooding also causes great loss of life and property.

Most of peninsular India is made up of the Deccan plateau. The Deccan and the hills along the coast are covered with tropical forests.

Asia is fringed by many important peninsulas and islands on which independent countries have been established. There are many bays and seas.

Covering so many degrees of latitude, the climate of Asia would naturally show great variation. There are great extremes of cold and heat in the Russian lowlands (Siberia) and northern China. The south is largely tropical. The heaviest rainfall anywhere is in some localities of southeastern Asia. All of the eastern region has enough rainfall for agriculture.

---

1. What is meant by the term "Eurasia"?
2. List six island countries of Asia.
3. What percentage of the world's land area does Asia occupy? What percentage of the world's population lives in Asia?
4. Asia has many great rivers. Name one that flows north, one that flows east, and one that flows south.

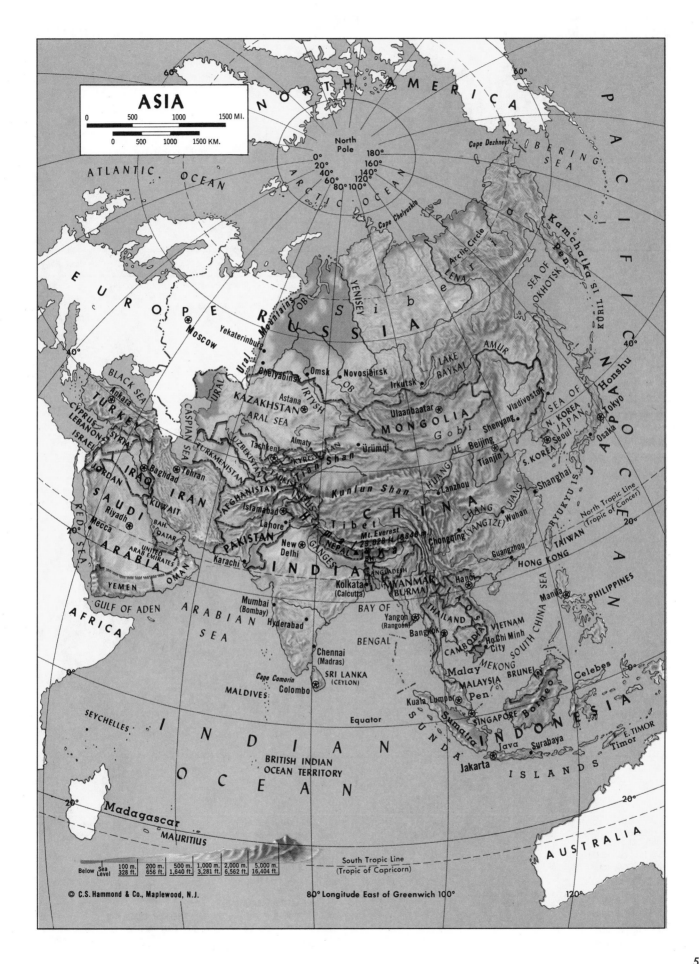

ASIA

0   500   1000   1500 MI.

0   500   1000   1500 KM.

ATLANTIC OCEAN

NORTH AMERICA

PACIFIC

North Pole

0° 20° 40° 60° 80° 100° 120° 140° 160° 180°

ARCTIC OCEAN

Cape Dezhnev

BERING SEA

Cape Chelyuskin

Arctic Circle

EUROPE

R U S S I A

S i b e r i a

LENA

YENISEY

OB

Kamchatka Pen.

SI

KURIL IS.

SEA OF OKHOTSK

40°

40°

Moscow

Yekaterinburg

Ural Mountains

URAL

Chelyabinsk

Omsk   Novosibirsk

OB   IRTYSH

Irkutsk

LAKE BAYKAL

AMUR

Vladivostok

SEA OF JAPAN

Honshu

BLACK SEA

Ankara

TURKEY

CYPRUS

LEBANON SYRIA

ISRAEL

CASPIAN SEA

KAZAKHSTAN

Astana

ARAL SEA

Almaty

Tashkent

UZBEKISTAN

TURKMENISTAN

KYRGYZSTAN

TAJIKISTAN

Tian Shan

Ürümqi

MONGOLIA

Ulaanbaatar

Gobi   Shenyang

HE   Beijing

N. KOREA

Seoul

S. KOREA

JAPAN

Tokyo

Osaka

JORDAN   IRAQ

Baghdad   Tehran

IRAN

KUWAIT

Islamabad

AFGHANISTAN

Lahore

Kunlun Shan

Tibet

C H I N A

Lanzhou

HUANG

Tianjin

Shanghai

RYUKYU IS.

North Tropic Line (Tropic of Cancer)

20°

SAUDI

Riyadh

BAH.

QATAR

Mecca

RED SEA

UNITED ARAB EMIRATES

OMAN

ARABIA

PAKISTAN

New Delhi

Karachi

GANGES

NEPAL

Mt. Everest 29,028 ft (8,848 m)

I N D I A

BANGLADESH

Kolkata (Calcutta)

HUANG

CHANG   Wuhan

YANGTZE

Chongqing

Guangzhou

HONG KONG

TAIWAN

PACIFIC OCEAN

20°

YEMEN

GULF OF ADEN

AFRICA

ARABIAN SEA

Mumbai (Bombay)

Hyderabad

BAY OF BENGAL

Yangon (Rangoon)

Bangkok

MYANMAR BURMA

Hanoi

LAOS

THAILAND

VIETNAM

Ho Chi Minh City

CAMBODIA

MEKONG

SOUTH CHINA SEA

Manila

PHILIPPINES

0°

Chennai (Madras)

SRI LANKA (CEYLON)

Cape Comorin   Colombo

MALDIVES

Malay Pen.

MALAYSIA

Kuala Lumpur

SINGAPORE

BRUNEI

Borneo

Celebes

I N D O N E S I A

E. TIMOR

Timor

0°

SEYCHELLES

I N D I A N

Equator

SUNDA

Sumatra

Java   Surabaya

O C E A N

BRITISH INDIAN OCEAN TERRITORY

Jakarta

ISLANDS

20°

Madagascar

MAURITIUS

South Tropic Line (Tropic of Capricorn)

AUSTRALIA

20°

Below Sea Level   100 m. 328 ft.   200 m. 656 ft.   500 m. 1,640 ft.   1,000 m. 3,281 ft.   2,000 m. 6,562 ft.   5,000 m. 16,404 ft.

© C.S. Hammond & Co., Maplewood, N.J.

80° Longitude East of Greenwich 100°

120°

55

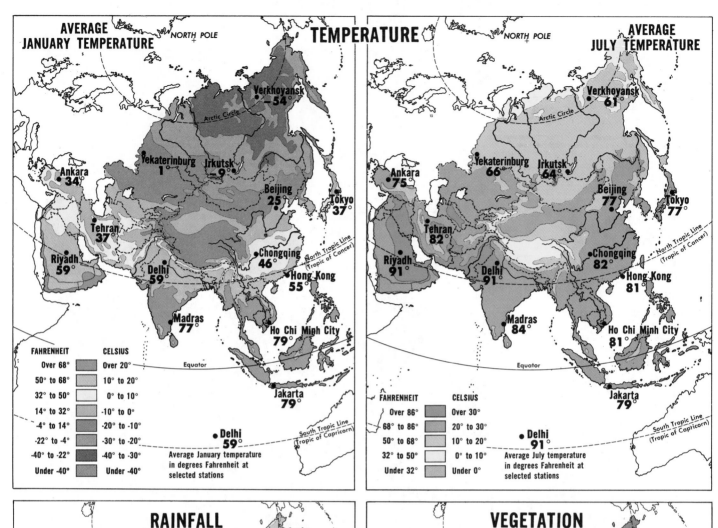

TEMPERATURE

AVERAGE JANUARY TEMPERATURE

NORTH POLE

Verkhoyansk −54°

Arctic Circle

Yekaterinburg 1°   Irkutsk −9°

Ankara 34°

Beijing 25°

Tokyo 37°

Tehran 37°

Chongqing 46°

North Tropic Line (Tropic of Cancer)

Riyadh 59°

Delhi 59°

Hong Kong 55°

Madras 77°

Ho Chi Minh City 79°

Equator

Jakarta 79°

South Tropic Line (Tropic of Capricorn)

● Delhi 59°

FAHRENHEIT	CELSIUS
Over 68°	Over 20°
50° to 68°	10° to 20°
32° to 50°	0° to 10°
14° to 32°	−10° to 0°
−4° to 14°	−20° to −10°
−22° to −4°	−30° to −20°
−40° to −22°	−40° to −30°
Under −40°	Under −40°

Average January temperature in degrees Fahrenheit at selected stations

AVERAGE JULY TEMPERATURE

NORTH POLE

Verkhoyansk 61°

Arctic Circle

Yekaterinburg 66°   Irkutsk 64°

Ankara 75°

Beijing 77°

Tokyo 77°

Tehran 82°

Chongqing 82°

North Tropic Line (Tropic of Cancer)

Riyadh 91°

Delhi 91°

Hong Kong 81°

Madras 84°

Ho Chi Minh City 81°

Equator

Jakarta 79°

South Tropic Line (Tropic of Capricorn)

● Delhi 91°

FAHRENHEIT	CELSIUS
Over 86°	Over 30°
68° to 86°	20° to 30°
50° to 68°	10° to 20°
32° to 50°	0° to 10°
Under 32°	Under 0°

Average July temperature in degrees Fahrenheit at selected stations

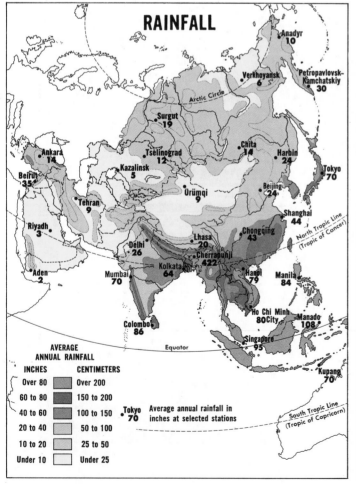

RAINFALL

Anadyr 10

Verkhoyansk 6

Petropavlovsk-Kamchatskiy 30

Arctic Circle

Surgut 19

Chita 14   Harbin 24

Tselinograd 12

Tokyo 70

Ankara 14

Kazalinsk 5

Beijing 24

Beirut 35

Ürümqi 9

Shanghai 44

Tehran 9

Lhasa 20   Chongqing 43

North Tropic Line (Tropic of Cancer)

Riyadh 3

Delhi 26

Cherrapunji 422

Hanoi 79   Manila 84

Aden 2

Kolkata 64

Mumbai 70

Ho Chi Minh 80 City   Manado 108

Colombo 86

Singapore 95

Equator

Kupang 70

AVERAGE ANNUAL RAINFALL

INCHES	CENTIMETERS
Over 80	Over 200
60 to 80	150 to 200
40 to 60	100 to 150
20 to 40	50 to 100
10 to 20	25 to 50
Under 10	Under 25

● Tokyo 70   Average annual rainfall in inches at selected stations

South Tropic Line (Tropic of Capricorn)

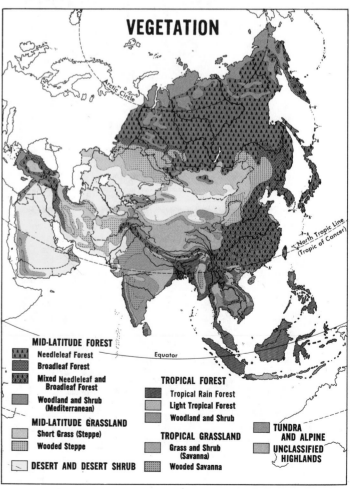

VEGETATION

Arctic Circle

North Tropic Line (Tropic of Cancer)

Equator

MID-LATITUDE FOREST
Needleleaf Forest
Broadleaf Forest
Mixed Needleleaf and Broadleaf Forest
Woodland and Shrub (Mediterranean)

MID-LATITUDE GRASSLAND
Short Grass (Steppe)
Wooded Steppe

DESERT AND DESERT SHRUB

TROPICAL FOREST
Tropical Rain Forest
Light Tropical Forest
Woodland and Shrub

TROPICAL GRASSLAND
Grass and Shrub (Savanna)
Wooded Savanna

TUNDRA AND ALPINE

UNCLASSIFIED HIGHLANDS

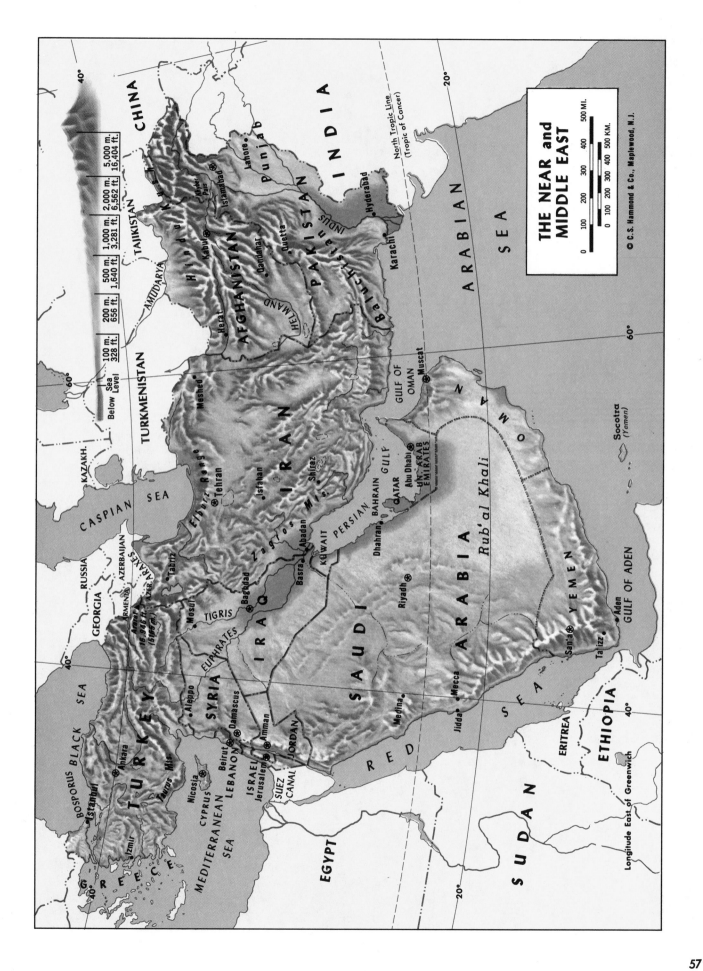

THE NEAR and
MIDDLE EAST

500 MI.
400
300
200
100
0

500 KM.
400
300
200
100
0

© C.S. Hammond & Co., Maplewood, N.J.

5,000 m. 16,404 ft.
2,000 m. 6,562 ft.
1,000 m. 3,281 ft.
500 m. 1,640 ft.
200 m. 656 ft.
100 m. 328 ft.
Sea Level
Below Sea Level

CHINA

TAJIKISTAN

TURKMENISTAN

KAZAKH.

AMUDARYA

Hindu Kush

AFGHANISTAN

Kabul
Khyber Pass
Kandahar
HELMAND

PAKISTAN

Punjab
Lahore
Islamabad
INDUS
Quetta
BALUCHISTAN
Hyderabad
Karachi

INDIA

North Tropic Line
(Tropic of Cancer)

ARABIAN
SEA

20°

60°

Socotra
(Yemen)

Meshed

Herat

IRAN

Tehran
Elburz Range
Isfahan
Shiraz
Zagros Mts.
Abadan
Basra
Baghdad
Mosul
TIGRIS
EUPHRATES
IRAQ
KUWAIT

Dhahran

BAHRAIN
QATAR
Abu Dhabi
UN. ARAB
EMIRATES

PERSIAN GULF

GULF OF
OMAN

Muscat

OMAN

Rub' al Khali

SAUDI

ARABIA

Riyadh

YEMEN

Aden
GULF OF ADEN
Sana
Taʿizz

CASPIAN SEA

RUSSIA
GEORGIA
ARMENIA
AZERBAIJAN
ARAXES
Ararat
16,945 ft.
(5165 m.)
Tabriz

Damascus
Aleppo
SYRIA
LEBANON
Beirut
ISRAEL
Jerusalem
Amman
JORDAN

Medina
Mecca
Jidda

RED
SEA

ERITREA
ETHIOPIA

40°

SUDAN

EGYPT

Longitude East of Greenwich

20°

TURKEY
Ankara
Taurus Mts.
Istanbul
BOSPORUS
BLACK SEA
Izmir
GREECE
G.
Nicosia
CYPRUS
MEDITERRANEAN SEA
SUEZ CANAL

40°

40°

40°

60°

60°

57

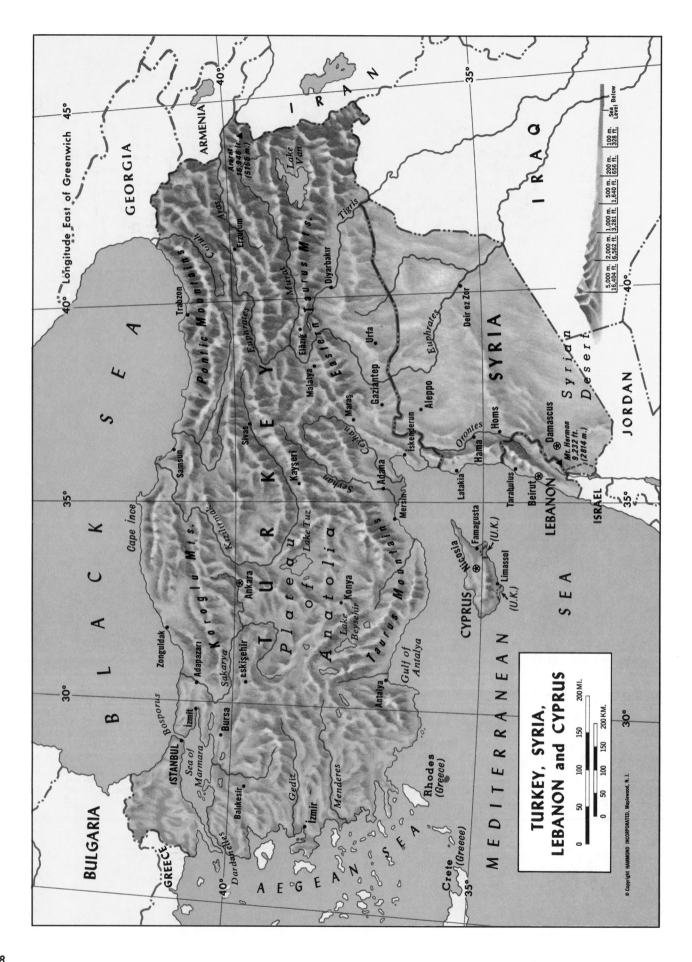

TURKEY, SYRIA, LEBANON and CYPRUS

© Copyright HAMMOND INCORPORATED, Maplewood, N.J.

Sea Level Below
100 m. 328 ft.
200 m. 656 ft.
500 m. 1,640 ft.
1,000 m. 3,281 ft.
2,000 m. 6,562 ft.
5,000 m. 16,404 ft.

200 MI.
0 50 100 150
0 50 100 150 200 KM.

GEORGIA

ARMENIA

IRAN

IRAQ

JORDAN

ISRAEL

LEBANON

SYRIA

CYPRUS

BULGARIA

GREECE

T U R K E Y

BLACK SEA

AEGEAN SEA

MEDITERRANEAN SEA

Longitude East of Greenwich

45°

40°

35°

Ararat 16,946 ft. (5165 m.) ▲

Lake Van

Tigris

Euphrates

Euphrates

Deir ez Zor

Syrian Desert

Damascus ⊛

Mt. Hermon 9,232 ft. (2814 m.)

Homs

Hama

Tarabulus

Beirut ⊛

Latakia

Orontes

Aleppo

Iskenderun

Urfa

Gaziantep

Maras

Adana

Mersin

Diyarbakır

Elazığ

Malatya

Erzurum

Çoruh

Ayas

Trabzon

Samsun

Sivas

Kayseri

 Pontic Mountains

Eastern Taurus Mts.

Murat

Ceyhan

Seyhan

Kızılırmak

Lake Tuz

Ankara ⊛

Konya

Lake Beyşehir

Plateau of Anatolia

Taurus Mountains

Antalya

Gulf of Antalya

Nicosia ⊛

Famagusta (U.K.)

Limassol (U.K.)

Zonguldak

Adapazarı

Eskişehir

Sakarya

Köroğlu Mts.

İzmit

Bursa

Balıkesir

İzmir

Gediz

Menderes

Rhodes (Greece)

Crete (Greece)

İstanbul

Bosporus

Sea of Marmara

Dardanelles

Cape İnce

40°

35°

30°

58

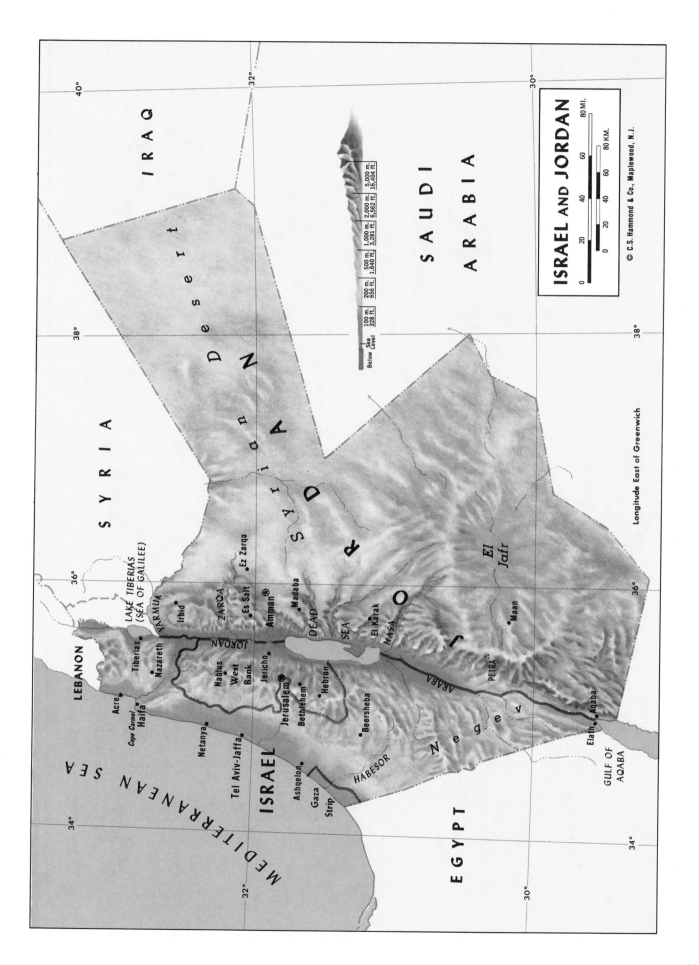

ISRAEL AND JORDAN

© C.S. Hammond & Co., Maplewood, N.J.

0   20   40   60   80 MI.

0   20   40   60   80 KM.

Sea Level
Below Sea Level
100 m. 328 ft.
200 m. 656 ft.
500 m. 1,640 ft.
1,000 m. 3,281 ft.
2,000 m. 6,562 ft.
5,000 m. 16,404 ft.

IRAQ

SYRIA

Syrian Desert

SAUDI ARABIA

JORDAN

El Jafr

Maan

PETRA

ARABA

HASA

El Karak

DEAD SEA

Madaba

Amman

Es Salt

ZARQA

Ez Zarqa

Irbid

YARMUK

LAKE TIBERIAS (SEA OF GALILEE)

Tiberias

Nazareth

JORDAN

Nablus

West Bank

Jericho

Jerusalem

Bethlehem

Hebron

Beersheba

Negev

HABESOR

Beersheba

LEBANON

Acre

Cape Carmel

Haifa

Netanya

Tel Aviv-Jaffa

Ashqelon

Gaza Strip

ISRAEL

MEDITERRANEAN SEA

EGYPT

Elath

Aqaba

GULF OF AQABA

Longitude East of Greenwich

40°   38°   36°   30°

32°   30°   34°

59

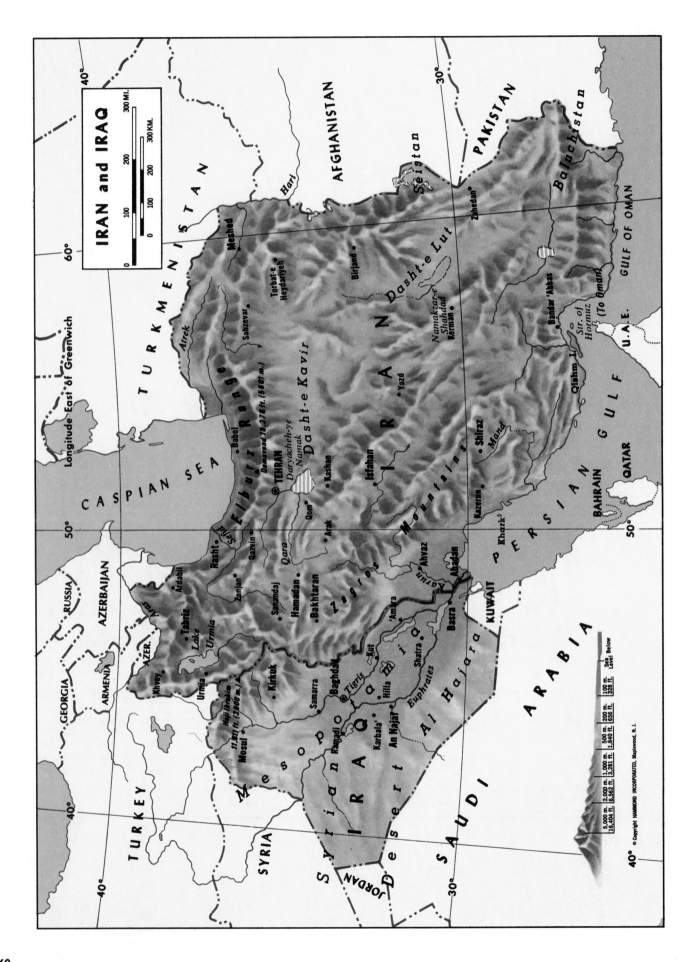

IRAN and IRAQ

300 MI.
300 KM.
200
100
0

GEORGIA
ARMENIA
AZERBAIJAN
AZER.
RUSSIA

TURKEY

Khvoy
Urmia
Lake
Urmia
Tabriz
Ardabil
Haji Ibrahim
11,811 ft. (3600 m.)
Mosul
Kirkuk
Zanjan
Sanandaj
Rawndiz
Hamadan
Bakhtaran
Zagros
Samarra

SYRIA

Syrian
Desert

Mesopotamia
I R A Q

Baghdad
Tigris
Kut
Hilla
Karbala'
An Najaf
Euphrates
Shatra
'Amara
Al Hajara

JORDAN

SAUDI ARABIA

KUWAIT

Basra
Abadan
Ahvaz
Karun

TURKMENISTAN

Longitude East of Greenwich

CASPIAN SEA

Atrek
Meshed
Babol
Sabzevar
Rasht
Sefid
Qazvin
Qara
Elburz Range
Damavand 18,376 ft. (5601 m.)
TEHRAN
Daryacheh-ye
Namak
Qom
Arak
Kashan
Dasht-e Kavir
Isfahan
I R A N
Torbat-e
Heydariyeh
Birjand

AFGHANISTAN

Hari

Seistan

PAKISTAN

Baluchistan

Zhedan

Dasht-e Lut
Namakzar-e
Shahdad
Kerman
Yazd
Shiraz
Mand
Kazerun

Mountains

Bandar 'Abbas
Qishm I.
Str. of
Hormuz
(To Oman)

GULF OF OMAN

U.A.E.

Khark I.
P E R S I A N   G U L F

BAHRAIN
QATAR

A R A B I A

5,000 m. | 2,000 m. | 1,000 m. | 500 m. | 200 m. | 100 m. | Sea
16,404 ft. | 6,562 ft. | 3,281 ft. | 1,640 ft. | 656 ft. | 328 ft. | Level   Below

© Copyright HAMMOND INCORPORATED, Maplewood, N.J.

60

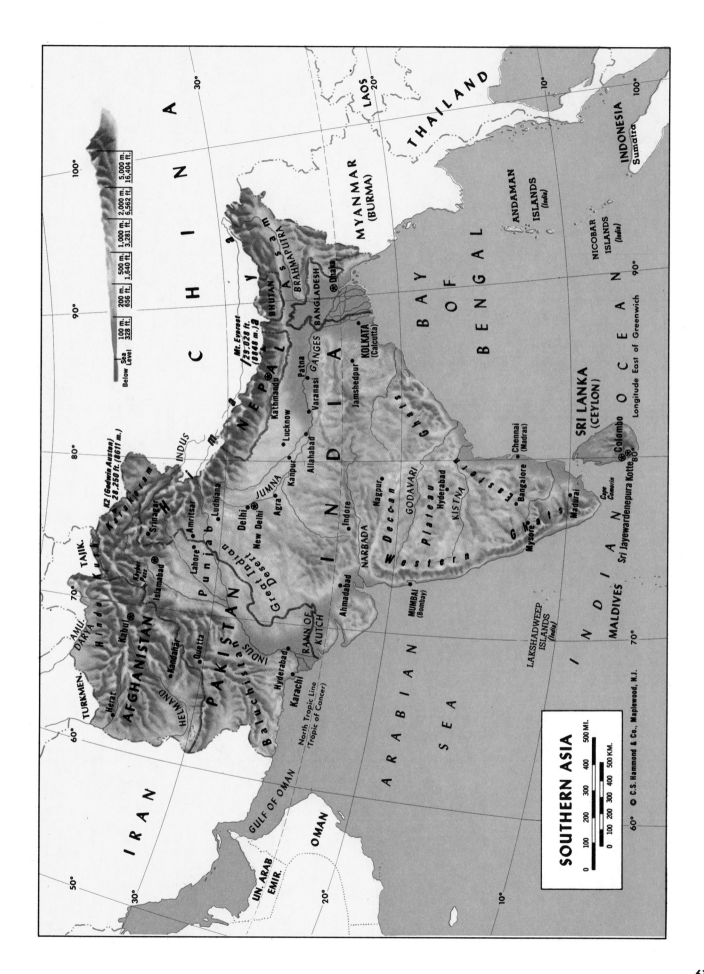

CHINA

TURKMEN.

TAJIK.

AMU.

DARYA

Hindu Kush

Khyber Pass

Kabul

Herat

Kandahar

AFGHANISTAN

HELMAND

Quetta

IRAN

Baluchistan

Hyderabad

Karachi

GULF OF OMAN

OMAN

UN. ARAB EMIR.

ARABIAN SEA

K2 (Godwin Austen) 28,250 ft. (8611 m.)

Karakoram

Srinagar

INDUS

Islamabad

Lahore

Amritsar

Ludhiana

Punjab

PAKISTAN

Indus

RANN OF KUTCH

North Tropic Line (Tropic of Cancer)

Ahmadabad

Indore

NARBADA

Great Indian Desert

Delhi

New Delhi

JUMNA

Agra

Kanpur

Allahabad

Lucknow

Varanasi

GANGES

Patna

Kathmandu

Mt. Everest 29,028 ft. (8848 m.)

NEPAL

Himalaya

BHUTAN

Assam

BRAHMAPUTRA

BANGLADESH

Dhaka

INDIA

MUMBAI (Bombay)

Nagpur

Deccan

Plateau

Western

GODAVARI

Hyderabad

KISTNA

Ghats

Eastern

Mysore

Bangalore

Chennai (Madras)

Ghats

Madurai

Cape Comorin

Jamshedpur

KOLKATA (Calcutta)

MYANMAR (BURMA)

THAILAND

LAOS

BAY

OF

BENGAL

ANDAMAN ISLANDS (India)

NICOBAR ISLANDS (India)

SRI LANKA (CEYLON)

Colombo

Sri Jayewardenepura Kotte

INDIAN

OCEAN

Longitude East of Greenwich

LAKSHADWEEP ISLANDS (India)

MALDIVES

INDONESIA

Sumatra

Below Sea Level | 100 m. 328 ft. | 200 m. 656 ft. | 500 m. 1,640 ft. | 1,000 m. 3,281 ft. | 2,000 m. 6,562 ft. | 5,000 m. 16,404 ft.

SOUTHERN ASIA

0 100 200 300 400 500 MI.

0 100 200 300 400 500 KM.

© C.S. Hammond & Co., Maplewood, N.J.

61

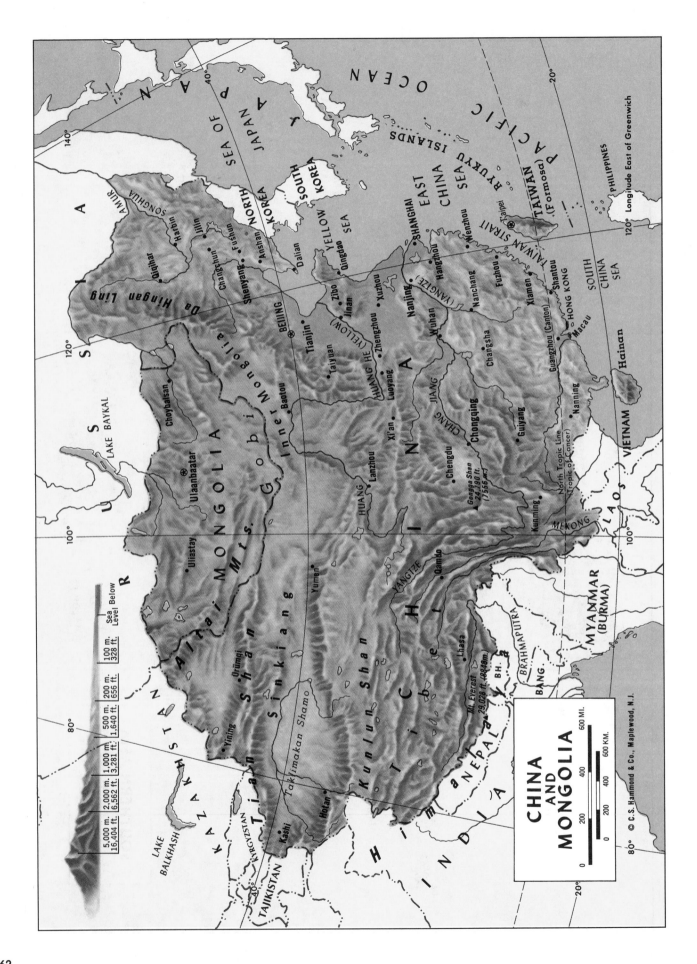

CHINA
AND
MONGOLIA

© C.S. Hammond & Co., Maplewood, N.J.

120° Longitude East of Greenwich

Scale legend:

5,000 m.	2,000 m.	1,000 m.	500 m.	200 m.	100 m.	Sea
16,404 ft.	6,562 ft.	3,281 ft.	1,640 ft.	656 ft.	328 ft.	Level Below

0   200   400   600 MI.
0   200   400   600 KM.

Map labels:

PACIFIC OCEAN

SEA OF JAPAN

JAPAN

NORTH KOREA

SOUTH KOREA

YELLOW SEA

EAST CHINA SEA

RYUKYU ISLANDS

TAIWAN (Formosa)

Taipei

TAIWAN STRAIT

SOUTH CHINA SEA

HONG KONG

Macau

Hainan

PHILIPPINES

VIETNAM

LAOS

MYANMAR (BURMA)

BANG.

BRAHMAPUTRA

INDIA

NEPAL

BH.

Himalaya

Mt. Everest 29,028 ft. (8,848 m.)

Lhasa

Tibet

Qamdo

Hotan

Kashi

Taklimakan Shamo

Sinkiang

Kunlun Shan

Tian Shan

Ürümqi

Yining

KAZAKSTAN

KYRGYZSTAN

TAJIKISTAN

LAKE BALKHASH

Altai Mts.

MONGOLIA

Uliastay

Ulaanbaatar

Choybalsan

LAKE BAYKAL

U S S R

Gobi Desert

Inner Mongolia

Baotou

Yumen

Lanzhou

Xi'an

HUANG

Chengdu

Chongqing

Gongga Shan 24,790 ft. (7,556 m.)

Guiyang

Kunming

MEKONG

North Tropic Line (Tropic of Cancer)

Nanning

Guangzhou (Canton)

Shantou

Xiamen

Fuzhou

Changsha

Nanchang

Wuhan

CHANG JIANG

YANGTZE

Nanjing

Hangzhou

Wenzhou

SHANGHAI

Xuzhou

Zhengzhou

Luoyang

HUANG HE (YELLOW)

Jinan

Zibo

Qingdao

Dalian

Tianjin

BEIJING

Taiyuan

Shenyang

Fushun

Anshan

Changchun

Jilin

Harbin

Qiqihar

Da Hingan Ling

SONGHUA

AMUR

CHINA

62

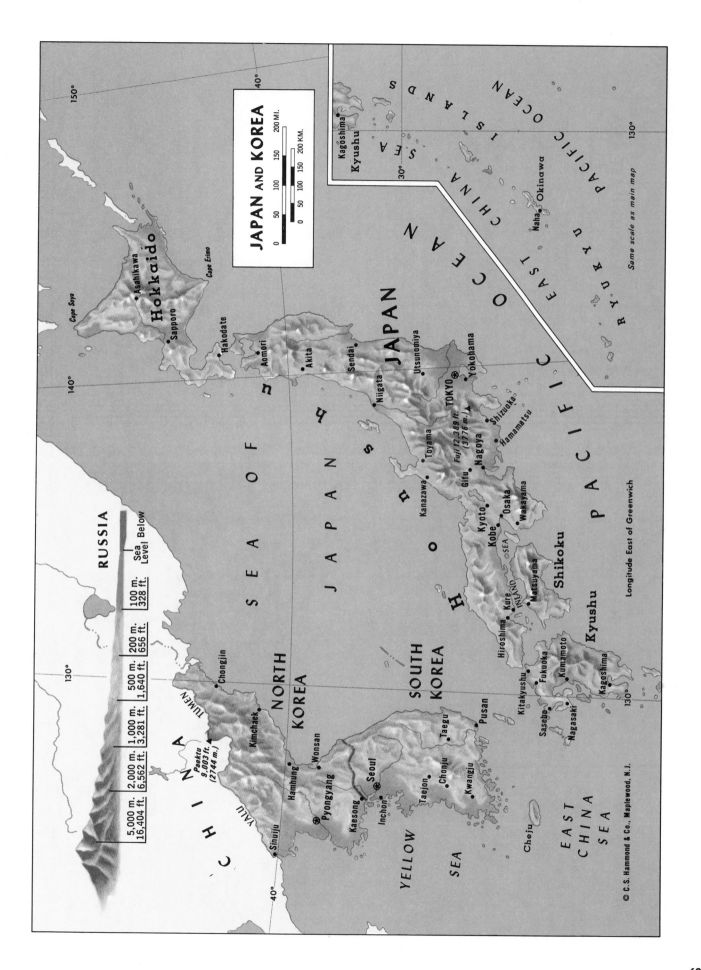

JAPAN AND KOREA

200 MI.
0 50 100 150
0 50 100 150 200 KM.

RUSSIA

| 5,000 m.
16,404 ft. | 2,000 m.
6,562 ft. | 1,000 m.
3,281 ft. | 500 m.
1,640 ft. | 200 m.
656 ft. | 100 m.
328 ft. | Sea
Level Below |

Same scale as main map

Longitude East of Greenwich

© C.S. Hammond & Co., Maplewood, N.J.

Hokkaido

Cape Soya
Asahikawa
Cape Erimo
Sapporo
Hakodate

Aomori
Akita
Sendai

JAPAN

Niigata
Utsunomiya
TOKYO
Yokohama

Toyama
Fuji 12,389 ft.
(3776 m.)
Nagoya
Shizuoka
Hamamatsu

Kanazawa
Gifu

Kyoto
Osaka
Kobe
Wakayama

Shikoku

Matsuyama

Hiroshima
Kure
INLAND
SEA

Kyushu

Kitakyushu
Fukuoka
Kumamoto
Sasebo
Nagasaki
Kagoshima

Kagoshima
Kyushu

Naha, Okinawa

RYUKYU ISLANDS

EAST CHINA SEA

PACIFIC OCEAN

SEA OF JAPAN

NORTH KOREA

Chongjin
Kimchaek
Wonsan
Hamhung
Pyongyang
Kaesong
Sinuiju

Paektu
9,003 ft.
(2744 m.)

TUMEN
YALU

CHINA

SOUTH KOREA

Seoul
Inchon
Taejon
Chonju
Kwangju
Taegu
Pusan

Cheju

YELLOW SEA

EAST CHINA SEA

63

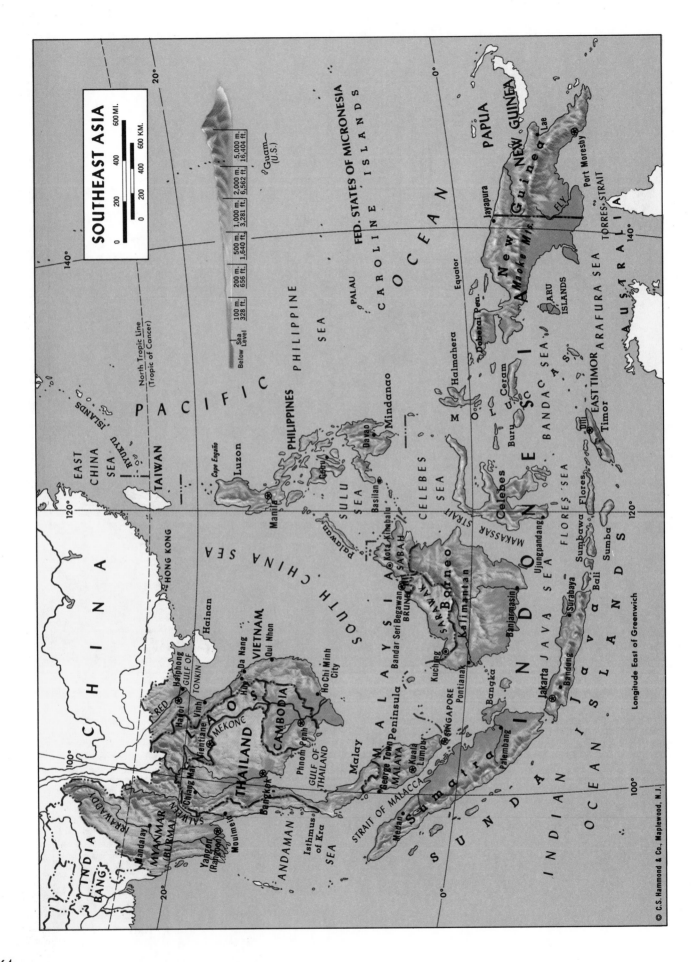

SOUTHEAST ASIA

0	200	400	600 MI.
0	200	400	600 KM.

Below Sea Level	Sea Level	
100 m. 328 ft.		
200 ft. 656 ft.		
500 m. 1,640 ft.		
1,000 m. 3,281 ft.		
2,000 m. 6,562 ft.		
5,000 m. 16,404 ft.		

PACIFIC OCEAN

CHINA

EAST CHINA SEA

RYUKYU ISLANDS

TAIWAN

HONG KONG

Hainan

GULF OF TONKIN

Haiphong
Hanoi
Vinh
RED
MEKONG
Nientiane
Chiang Mai
LAO
VIETNAM
Da Nang
Hue
Qui Nhon
Ho Chi Minh City
Phnom Penh
CAMBODIA
THAILAND
SALWEEN
Bangkok
GULF OF THAILAND

MYANMAR (BURMA)
IRRAWADDY
Mandalay
Yangon (Rangoon)
Moulmein
Isthmus of Kra
ANDAMAN SEA

INDIA
BANG.

Malay
Malay Peninsula
George Town
MALAYA
Kuala Lumpur
SINGAPORE
STRAIT OF MALACCA
Medan

SOUTH CHINA SEA

Palawan

MALAYSIA
SARAWAK
Kuching
Pontianak
Bangka
Palembang
Sumatra

Kota Kinabalu
SABAH
BRUNEI
Bandar Seri Begawan
Borneo
Kalimantan
Banjarmasin

PHILIPPINES

Cape Engaño
Luzon
Cebu
Manila
Basilan
SULU SEA

Davao
Mindanao

PHILIPPINE SEA

PALAU

CAROLINE ISLANDS

FED. STATES OF MICRONESIA

Guam (U.S.)

North Tropic Line (Tropic of Cancer)

CELEBES SEA

Celebes

MAKASSAR STRAIT

JAVA SEA
Jakarta
Bandung
Surabaya
Java
Bali
Bandung

INDONESIA

FLORES SEA
Sumbawa
Flores
Sumba

Halmahera

Buru
Ceram

Doberai Pen.

BANDA SEA

ARU ISLANDS

ARAFURA SEA

EAST TIMOR
Timor

SUNDA ISLANDS

INDIAN OCEAN

Longitude East of Greenwich

PAPUA NEW GUINEA

New Guinea
Jayapura
Maoke Mts.
Lae
FLY
Port Moresby
TORRES STRAIT

Equator

AUSTRALIA

© C.S. Hammond & Co., Maplewood, N.J.

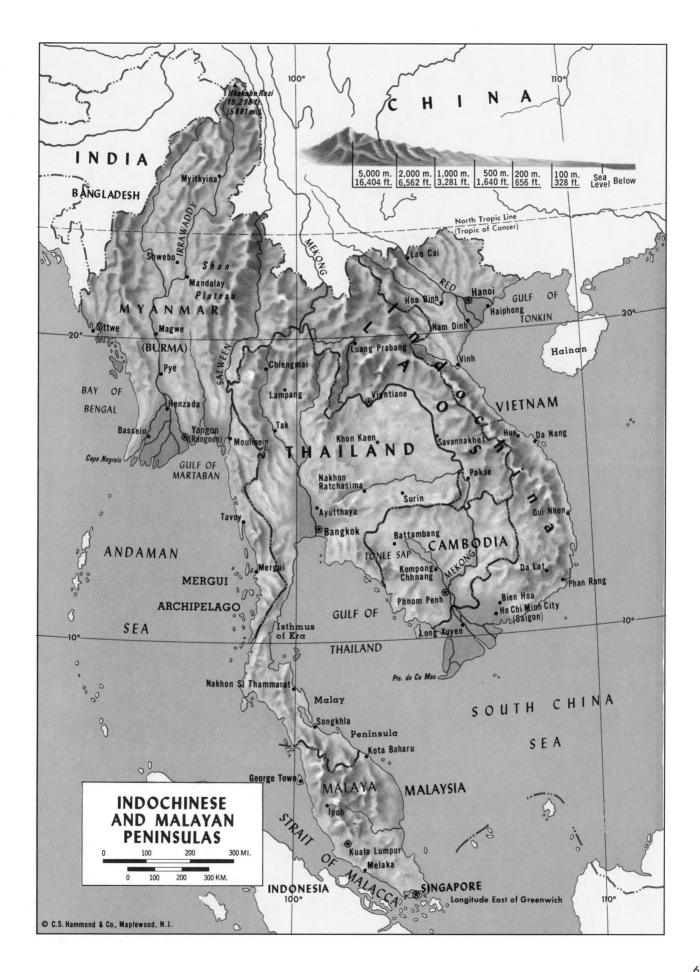

INDOCHINESE AND MALAYAN PENINSULAS

CHINA

5,000 m. | 2,000 m. | 1,000 m. | 500 m. | 200 m. | 100 m. | Sea
16,404 ft. | 6,562 ft. | 3,281 ft. | 1,640 ft. | 656 ft. | 328 ft. | Level | Below

INDIA

BANGLADESH

Hkakabo Razi
19,296 ft.
(5881 m.)

Myitkyina

North Tropic Line
(Tropic of Cancer)

IRRAWADDY

MEKONG

Lao Cai

RED

Shwebo

Shan

Mandalay
Plateau

MYANMAR

Hoa Binh

Hanoi
Haiphong

GULF OF
TONKIN

20°

Nam Dinh

20°

Sittwe

Magwe

(BURMA)

Luang Prabang

Vinh

Hainan

Pye

Chiengmai

SALWEEN

Indochina

VIETNAM

BAY OF
BENGAL

Henzada

Lampang

Vientiane

Tak

Hue

Da Nang

Bassein

Yangon
(Rangoon)

Moulmein

Khon Kaen

Savannakhet

Cape Negrais

GULF OF
MARTABAN

THAILAND

Pakse

Qui Nhon

Nakhon
Ratchasima

Surin

ANDAMAN

Tavoy

Ayutthaya

Bangkok

Battambang

CAMBODIA

Da Lat

Phan Rang

MERGUI

Mergui

TONLE SAP

MEKONG

Bien Hoa

ARCHIPELAGO

Kompong
Chhnang

Ho Chi Minh City
(Saigon)

SEA

Phnom Penh

10°

Isthmus
of Kra

GULF OF

Long Xuyen

10°

THAILAND

SOUTH CHINA

Pte. de Ca Mau

Nakhon Si Thammarat

Malay

SEA

Songkhla

Peninsula

Kota Baharu

George Town

MALAYA

MALAYSIA

Ipoh

STRAIT

Kuala Lumpur

Melaka

OF

INDONESIA
100°

MALACCA

SINGAPORE

Longitude East of Greenwich

110°

**INDOCHINESE
AND MALAYAN
PENINSULAS**

0   100   200   300 MI.

0   100   200   300 KM.

© C.S. Hammond & Co., Maplewood, N.J.

65

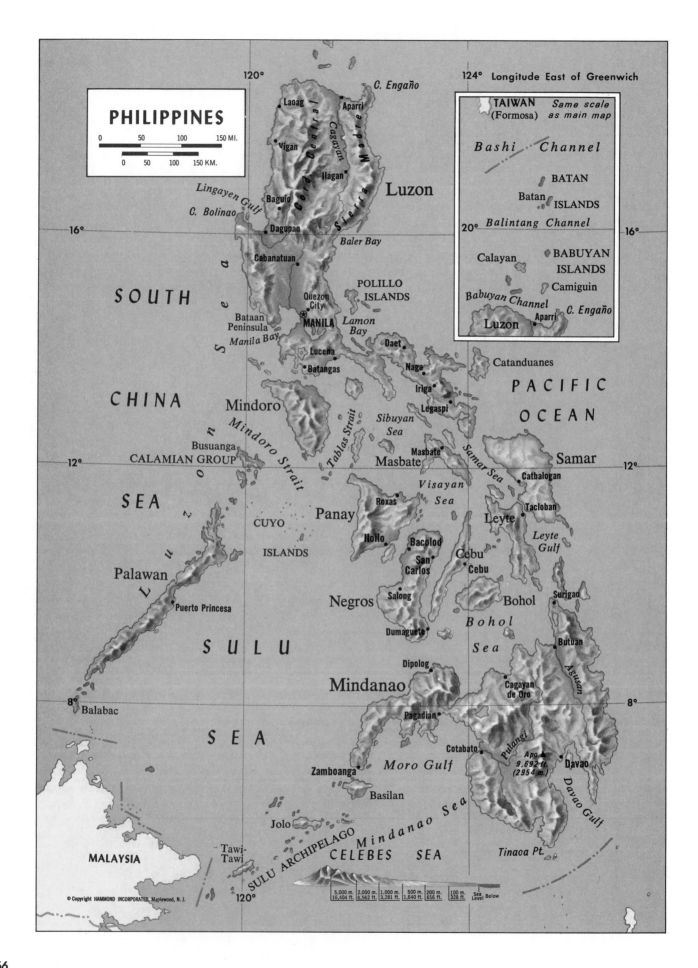

PHILIPPINES

0   50   100   150 MI.

0   50   100   150 KM.

120°

124° Longitude East of Greenwich

C. Engaño

Laoag
Aparri

Vigan

Cagayan

Cord. Central

Sierra Madre

Luzon

Ilagan

Baguio

Lingayen Gulf

C. Bolinao

Dagupan

16°

Baler Bay

Cabanatuan

SOUTH

POLILLO
ISLANDS

Quezon
City

*Lamon
Bay*

Bataan
Peninsula

⊛ MANILA

Lucena

Daet

CHINA

Manila Bay

Batangas

Naga

Catanduanes

Iriga

Mindoro

Legaspi

PACIFIC

*Sibuyan
Sea*

Busuanga

Mindoro Strait

OCEAN

CALAMIAN GROUP

12°

Tablas Strait

Masbate

Samar Sea

Samar

Masbate

SEA

CUYO

Panay

*Visayan
Sea*

Catbalogan

Roxas

12°

Palawan

ISLANDS

Iloilo

Tacloban

Leyte

Bacolod

Cebu

*Leyte
Gulf*

San
Carlos

Cebu

L u z o n

S e a

Puerto Princesa

Negros

Salong

Bohol

Surigao

SULU

Dumaguete

Bohol

Sea

Butuan

Dipolog

Agusan

Balabac

8°

Mindanao

Cagayan
de Oro

8°

SEA

Pagadian

Pulangi

Cotabato

Apo ▲
9,692 ft.
(2954 m.)

Davao

Zamboanga

Moro Gulf

Davao Gulf

Basilan

Mindanao Sea

Jolo

MALAYSIA

Tawi-
Tawi

SULU ARCHIPELAGO

CELEBES   SEA

Tinaca Pt.

© Copyright HAMMOND INCORPORATED, Maplewood, N.J.

120°

Inset: TAIWAN (Formosa) — Same scale as main map

TAIWAN
(Formosa)

*Same scale
as main map*

Bashi   Channel

BATAN

Batan

ISLANDS

20°

Balintang Channel

Calayan

BABUYAN
ISLANDS

Babuyan Channel

Camiguin

Luzon

Aparri

C. Engaño

16°

5,000 m.
16,404 ft. | 2,000 m.
6,562 ft. | 1,000 m.
3,281 ft. | 500 m.
1,640 ft. | 200 m.
656 ft. | 100 m.
328 ft. | Sea
Level | Below

AUSTRALIA AND NEW ZEALAND

Australia is the world's smallest continent. It lies entirely below the equator and for that reason is sometimes referred to as the continent "down under."

For the most part Australia has a regular coastline. Only the Gulf of Carpentaria in the north and the Great Australian Bight in the south cut deeply into the land. The Great Barrier Reef, the longest coral reef in the world, stretches for 1,250 miles (2,012 kilometers) off the northeast coast. Actually the reef is made up of many reefs and small islands.

A few miles inland from the east coast is an area of low mountain ranges and tablelands, known as the Eastern Highlands, or the Great Dividing Range. These ranges divide the heavily populated coastal plains from the less populated plains of the interior. Most of Australia's industry is located in the eastern coastal plains. The Eastern Highlands are low, with most of them under 3,000 feet (910 meters) above sea level. The mountains in the more rugged southeastern section are somewhat higher. Mt. Kosciusko, Australia's highest point, is found here. The island of Tasmania, 150 miles (240 kilometers) to the southeast, is a continuation of these highlands.

A second major region, the Central Lowlands, covers about one-third of the continent. It extends from the Gulf of Carpentaria in the north to the eastern shore of the Great Australian Bight in the south. Scientists think that these lowlands were once covered with water. Beneath the lowlands are several artesian basins—areas of underground water. One of them, the Great Artesian Basin, underlies about one-fifth of Australia and is the largest artesian basin in the world. The water cannot be used for continuous irrigation, but it does provide water for cattle and sheep. Much of this region is dry but there are large areas of grassland in the east. The Murray-Darling river system in the southeastern part of the region is the major river system in Australia. There are several large irrigation projects along the rivers. Their valleys are among the most productive farming and grazing areas in the country. Although the Australian economy is highly industrialized, livestock is an important part of the economy.

A third region, the Western Plateau, is in the western two-thirds of the continent. It is an area of desert and semidesert land. Most of the plateau is below 1,000 feet (305 meters) above sea level. Three very large deserts—the Gibson, Great Sandy, and Great Victoria deserts—are located here. The plateau is rimmed by steep cliffs, except in a few areas where it drops gently to the sea. In the south, the Nullarbor Plain is an unusual area below the cliffs. It is a remarkable smooth, barren lowland riddled by numerous underground caves. The rest of the plateau is edged by a narrow coastal plain. Although most of the Western Plateau is not suited to agriculture, it is rich in minerals.

Australia's climate is generally mild throughout the year. Although there is a rainy season from January to about April, most of the continent does not receive enough rain. Parts of it receive less than 10 inches (25 centimeters) a year. One of the striking things about Australia's weather is its changeability, especially in the south. For a short time each year, the winds will abruptly change direction, temperatures will rise or fall, or it will suddenly rain or stop raining.

Because so much of the interior is dry, most of Australia's major cities are located along the coast. Much of the transportation between cities is by ship, and all of the state capitals are seaports.

New Zealand is situated about 1,200 miles (1,930 kilometers) southeast of Australia. The nation has two main islands, North Island and South Island.

New Zealand is a mountainous country known for its beautiful scenery. North Island is of volcanic origin and some of its volcanoes are still active. The hills are covered with forests, but many of them have been cut down. North Island also has many hot springs, boiling mud, geysers, lakes of different colors, and waterfalls. A high mountain range called the Southern Alps runs along most of the length of South Island. Much of the land is fertile and is used for growing crops and raising sheep and cattle. Most of the cattle are found on North Island and the sheep on South Island.

New Zealand has several rivers but few are long or deep enough to be used for transportation. They are used for water power, however.

The climate of New Zealand is temperate, with mild winters and warm summers. It is warmest in the north and it gets increasingly colder to the south. Temperatures are lower at higher altitudes. Rainfall is heavy in most areas, especially on the west coast of South Island, where it sometimes reaches 250 inches (635 centimeters) a year in parts of the Southern Alps.

1. What is the Great Barrier Reef?
2. What are the three major land regions of Australia?
3. What is the Great Dividing Range?
4. Why is the Murray-Darling river system the most important drainage system in the country?
5. What large islands make up the nation of New Zealand?
6. Why do you think the climate of New Zealand is warmest in the north and colder to the south?

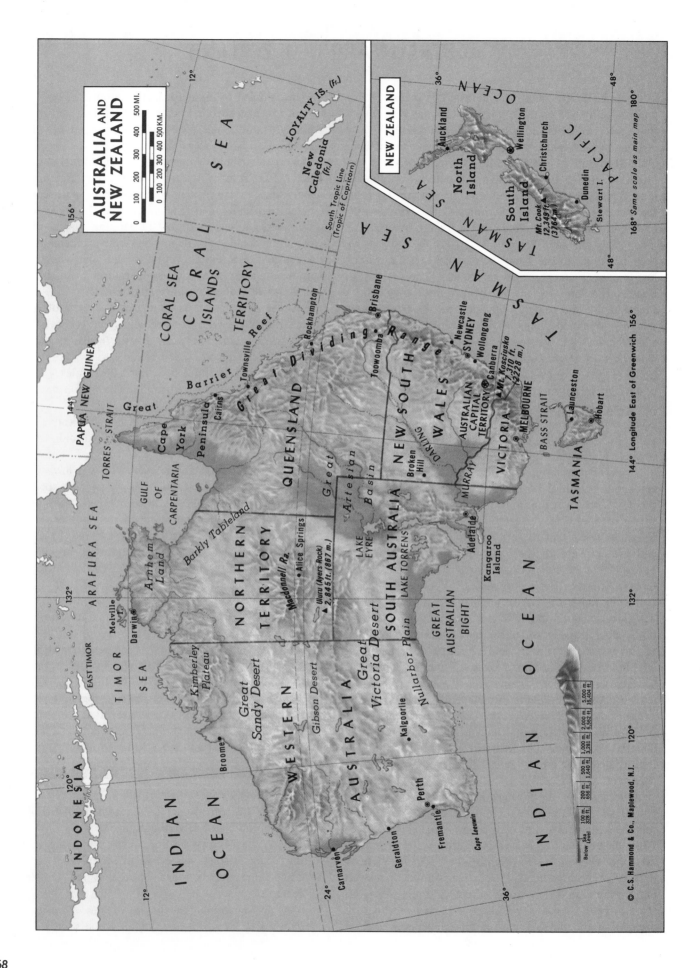

AUSTRALIA AND
NEW ZEALAND

500 MI.
400
300
200
100
0
0 100 200 300 400 500 KM.

NEW ZEALAND

OCEAN

36°

48°

Auckland

North
Island

Wellington

Christchurch

South
Island

Dunedin

Mt. Cook
12,349 ft.
(3764 m)

Stewart I.

P A C I F I C

TASMAN SEA

168° Same scale as main map 180°

S E A

LOYALTY IS. (Fr.)

New
Caledonia
(Fr.)

South Tropic Line
(Tropic of Capricorn)

CORAL SEA C O R A L
ISLANDS
TERRITORY

Barrier

Great

Townsville Reef

Rockhampton

Toowoomba

Brisbane

Newcastle

SYDNEY

Wollongong

Canberra

AUSTRALIAN
CAPITAL
TERRITORY

Mt. Kosciusko
7,310 ft.
(2228 m.)

MELBOURNE

BASS STRAIT

Launceston

Hobart

T A S M A N   S E A

144° Longitude East of Greenwich 156°

PAPUA NEW GUINEA

TORRES   STRAIT

ARAFURA SEA

GULF
OF
CARPENTARIA

Cape
York
Peninsula

Cairns

QUEENSLAND

Great
Dividing
Range

N E W   S O U T H   W A L E S

DARLING

Broken
Hill

MURRAY

VICTORIA

TASMANIA

Great

Artesian

Basin

Barkly Tableland

Arnhem
Land

Melville
I.

Darwin

NORTHERN
TERRITORY

Macdonnell Ra.

Alice Springs

Uluru (Ayers Rock)
2,845 ft. (867 m.)

LAKE
EYRE

LAKE TORRENS

S O U T H   A U S T R A L I A

Adelaide

Kangaroo
Island

Murray

GREAT
AUSTRALIAN
BIGHT

TIMOR

SEA

Kimberley
Plateau

Great
Sandy Desert

Gibson Desert

Great
Victoria Desert

W E S T E R N

A U S T R A L I A

Nullarbor Plain

Kalgoorlie

Broome

Geraldton

Perth

Fremantle

Cape Leeuwin

Carnarvon

EAST TIMOR

I N D O N E S I A

I N D I A N

O C E A N

I N D I A N   O C E A N

100 m. 200 m. 500 m. 1,000 m. 2,000 m. 5,000 m.
328 ft. 656 ft. 1,640 ft. 3,281 ft. 6,562 ft. 16,404 ft.

Below Sea
Level

© C.S. Hammond & Co., Maplewood, N.J.

156°

12°

144°

132°

120°

12°

24°

36°

132°

120°

36°

48°

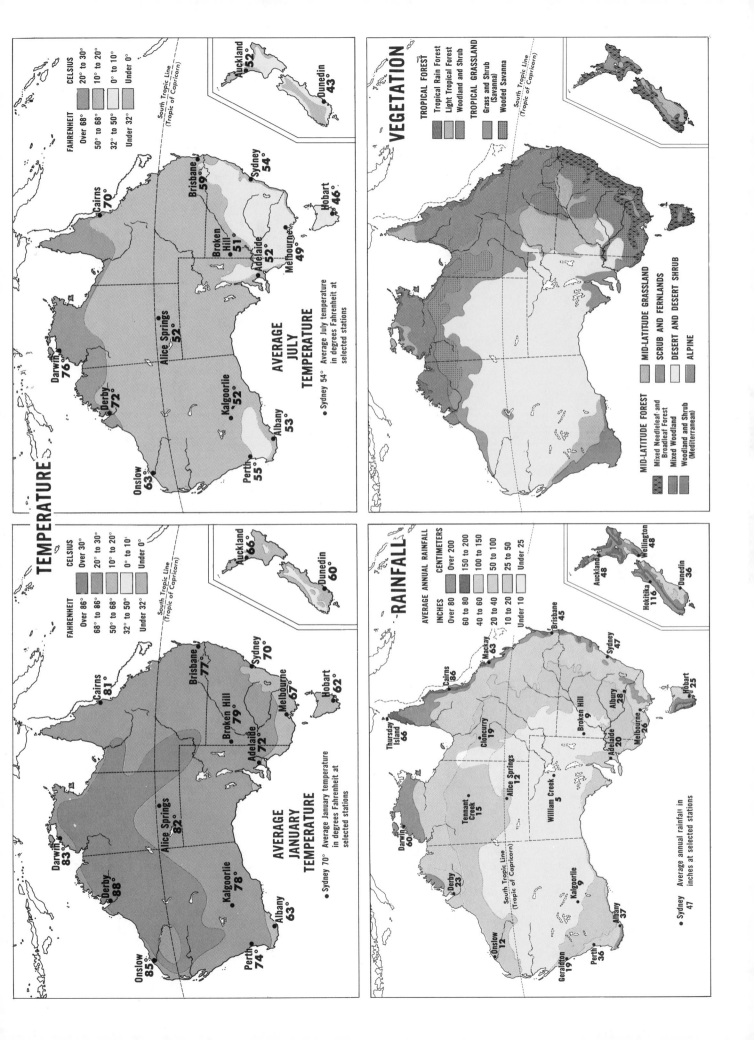

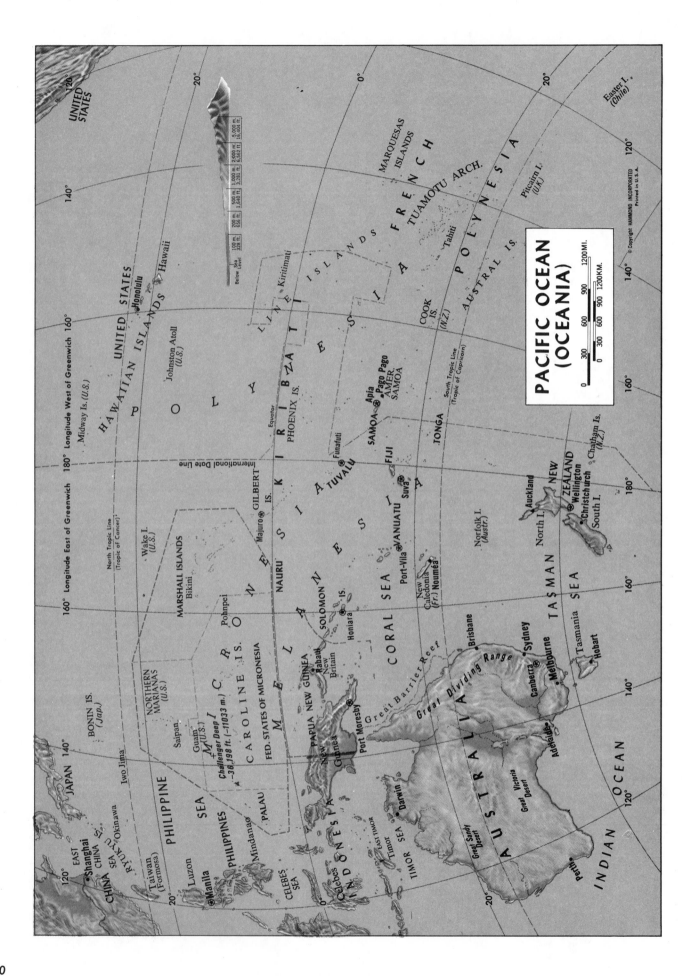

PACIFIC OCEAN
(OCEANIA)

0 300 600 900 1200 MI.
0 300 600 900 1200 KM.

© Copyright HAMMOND INCORPORATED   Printed in U.S.A.

Below Sea Level
Sea Level | 100 m. 328 ft. | 200 m. 656 ft. | 500 m. 1,640 ft. | 1,000 m. 3,281 ft. | 2,000 m. 6,562 ft. | 5,000 m. 16,404 ft.

Easter I. (Chile)

UNITED STATES

MARQUESAS ISLANDS

Pitcairn I. (U.K.)

TUAMOTU ARCH.

F R E N C H

P O L Y N E S I A

Tahiti

AUSTRAL IS.

COOK IS. (N.Z.)

HAWAIIAN ISLANDS   UNITED STATES

Hawaii

Honolulu

Midway Is. (U.S.)

Johnston Atoll (U.S.)

LINE ISLANDS

Kiritimati

P   O   L   Y   N   E   S   I   A

North Tropic Line (Tropic of Cancer)

International Date Line

Equator

PHOENIX IS.

Funafuti

SAMOA Apia

Pago Pago AMER. SAMOA

South Tropic Line (Tropic of Capricorn)

TONGA

FIJI

Suva

TUVALU

K   I   R   I   B   A   T   I

GILBERT IS.

Majuro

VANUATU

Port-Vila

New Caledonia (Fr.) Nouméa

M   E   L   A   N   E   S   I   A

CORAL SEA

Norfolk I. (Austr.)

Chatham Is. (N.Z.)

NEW ZEALAND

Auckland

North I.

Wellington

Christchurch

South I.

TASMAN SEA

MARSHALL ISLANDS

Bikini

Wake I. (U.S.)

NAURU

M   I   C   R   O   N   E   S   I   A

CAROLINE IS.

Pohnpei

FED. STATES OF MICRONESIA

SOLOMON IS.

Honiara

Rabaul   New Britain

PAPUA NEW GUINEA

New Guinea

Port Moresby

Great Barrier Reef

Brisbane

Great Dividing Range

Sydney

Canberra

Melbourne

Tasmania

Hobart

A   U   S   T   R   A   L   I   A

Great Victoria Desert

Adelaide

Great Sandy Desert

Darwin

Perth

INDIAN OCEAN

NORTHERN MARIANAS (U.S.)

Saipan

Guam (U.S.)

Challenger Deep −36,198 ft. (−11,033 m.)

PALAU

BONIN IS. (Jap.)

Iwo Jima

JAPAN

East CHINA SEA

Shanghai

Okinawa

RYUKYU IS.

CHINA

Taiwan (Formosa)

PHILIPPINE SEA

Luzon

PHILIPPINES

Manila

Mindanao

CELEBES SEA

I   N   D   O   N   E   S   I   A

Celebes

EAST TIMOR

Timor

TIMOR SEA

160° Longitude East of Greenwich

180° Longitude West of Greenwich

160°

140°

120°

100°

20°

0°

20°

70

OCEANIA

Oceania is the name of the 25,000 or more islands scattered across the Pacific Ocean. Some of the islands are little more than bits of rocks and sand. Others are much larger and are crowded with people. The people of Oceania speak many different languages. Until recently they lived isolated from the rest of the world.

The islands of Oceania were formed in two ways. Some are the result of erupting volcanoes. Flowing lava cooled around the volcanoes and built up land. Because volcanic soil is fertile, the mountainous or hilly lands of these islands are covered with trees and other plant life. The other kind of Pacific island was formed by the piling up of coral until a reef of land was formed. These coral reefs usually enclose a body of water, called a *lagoon,* in the center. Such coral islands are called *atolls.* They are low-lying islands with poor soil.

The Pacific islands are often divided into three groups — Polynesia, Micronesia, and Melanesia. The largest of the groups is Polynesia. The word "Polynesia" means "many islands." This group is in the shape of a huge triangle in the central Pacific. The southwestern corner of the triangle is at New Zealand. Its western boundary extends northward through the Tonga Islands and along the International Date Line to Midway Island. The boundary then runs southeast through the Hawaiian Islands to its point at Easter Island. From there it turns back to New Zealand. Most of the islands of Polynesia are mountainous and covered with thick forests.

Micronesia means "small islands." This group lies in the western Pacific between the equator and Japan. They stretch from the Philippines eastward to Polynesia. Micronesia includes the Mariana, Caroline, Marshall, Gilbert (Kiribati), and Ellice (Tuvalu) islands. Most are volcanic islands.

The third group, Melanesia, is just south of Micronesia. Melanesia means "black islands." These islands lie northeast of Australia and extend from New Guinea eastward to the Fiji Islands. The Melanesian islands are mostly mountainous and heavily forested.

Since most of Oceania is within the tropics, the climate of the region is hot and humid. The heat is made bearable, however, by cool ocean breezes. There is little change in season, and the year is divided into periods of greater and lesser rainfall.

A few islands, such as New Caledonia, Fiji, and the New Hebrides (Vanuatu), have rich mineral resources. On all, agriculture provides a living for its inhabitants.

1. What is another name for the Pacific Islands?
2. What are the three main island groups?
3. What is an atoll?

ANTARCTICA MAP—PAGE 72

Antarctica is the huge continent covered with ice and snow that surrounds the South Pole. Over the centuries the ice and snow have built up over the land until they cover about 95 percent of it. This giant mass of ice has made Antarctica the highest continent, with its general elevation around 7,500 feet (2,286 meters) above sea level. This ice also covers most of the coastline and in some places extends into the ocean, forming huge shelves of ice.

Antarctica is roughly circular in shape. Only the Weddell Sea and the Ross Sea extend any distance inland. Most of the continent is a plateau. The Transantarctic Mountains, a series of ranges running from Victoria Land to Coats Land, divide the continent into two regions—the East Antarctic and the West Antarctic.

East Antarctica, that portion south of the Indian Ocean and facing Africa and Australia, is the larger of the two regions. It is a high plateau that is one of the world's driest areas. West Antarctica, facing South America and the Pacific Ocean, is made up of a series of mountain ranges. One part of this region, the Antarctic Peninsula, is a long, mountainous ridge that stretches northward toward South America for about 1,200 miles (1,930 kilometers). The peninsula resembles the Andes and is probably part of the same mountain chain. If the ice were to melt, the peninsula would be seen to resemble southern Chile and to have many islands and deep fiords. Many of the peaks that can be seen above the ice cap are volcanoes, and at least two of them are still active. Vinson Massif, 16,864 feet (5,140 meters) above sea level is the continent's highest point.

Antarctica is the coldest, windiest, and the most barren of all the continents. No trees grow here. In only a few places will a few plants grow for a very short period of time each year.

1. Describe the two regions of Antarctica.
2. Name four countries that have stations in Antarctica.

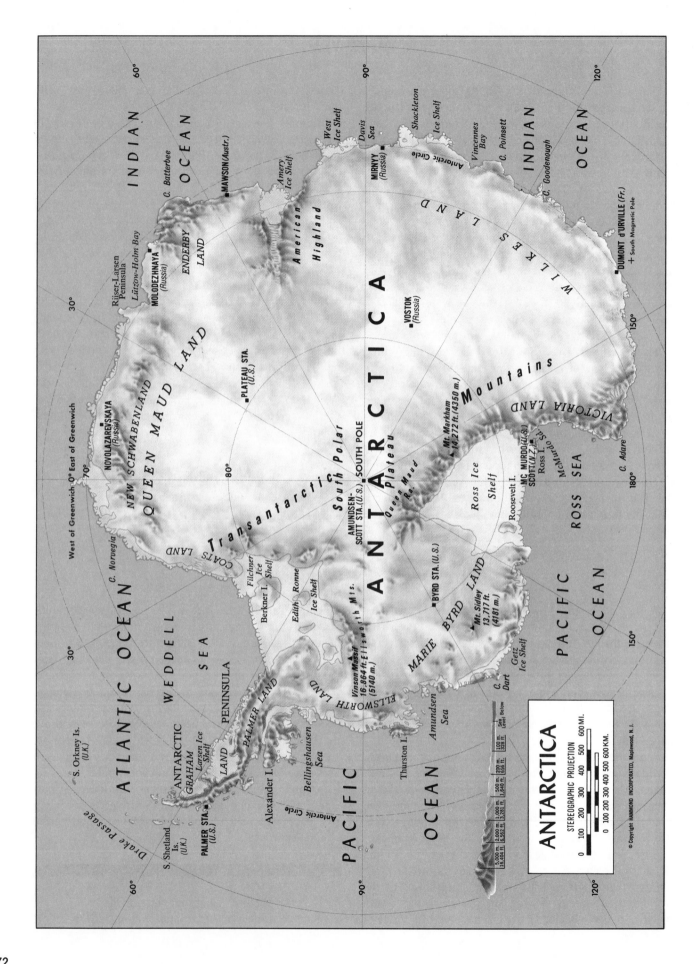

ATLANTIC OCEAN

INDIAN OCEAN

INDIAN OCEAN

S. Orkney Is. (U.K.)

Drake Passage

S. Shetland Is. (U.K.)

C. Batterbee

West Ice Shelf

Davis Sea

Shackleton Ice Shelf

Vincennes Bay

C. Poinsett

C. Goodenough

DUMONT d'URVILLE (Fr.)

+ South Magnetic Pole

C. Norvegia

West of Greenwich. 0° East of Greenwich

Riiser-Larsen Peninsula

Lützow-Holm Bay

MOLODEZHNAYA (Russia)

NOVOLAZAREVSKAYA (Russia)

MAWSON (Austr.)

Amery Ice Shelf

ENDERBY LAND

American Highland

MIRNY (Russia)

Antarctic Circle

VOSTOK (Russia)

WILKES LAND

NEW SCHWABENLAND

QUEEN MAUD LAND

PLATEAU STA. (U.S.)

30°

60°

70°

80°

90°

Mountains

VICTORIA LAND

C. Adare

C. Goodenough

COATS LAND

Filchner Ice Shelf

Berkner I. Shelf

Edith Ronne Ice Shelf

Transantarctic

South Polar Plateau

SOUTH POLE

AMUNDSEN-SCOTT STA. (U.S.)

ANTARCTICA

Queen Maud Ra.

Mt. Markham 14,272 ft. (4350 m.)

Ross Ice Shelf

Roosevelt I.

Ross I.

McMurdo

MC MURDO (U.S.)

SCOTT (N.Z.)

ROSS SEA

PACIFIC OCEAN

WEDDELL SEA

ANTARCTIC PENINSULA

GRAHAM LAND

Larsen Ice Shelf

PALMER STA. (U.S.)

PALMER LAND

Alexander I.

Antarctic Circle

Bellingshausen Sea

Thurston I.

Amundsen Sea

ELLSWORTH LAND

Vinson Massif 16,864 ft. Ellsworth Mts. (5140 m.)

BYRD STA. (U.S.)

MARIE BYRD LAND

Mt. Sidley 13,717 ft. (4181 m.)

C. Dart

Getz Ice Shelf

PACIFIC OCEAN

90°

120°

150°

180°

150°

120°

30°

60°

ANTARCTICA

STEREOGRAPHIC PROJECTION

0 100 200 300 400 500 600 MI.

0 100 200 300 400 500 600 KM.

5,000 ft. 16,404 ft. | 2,000 m. 6,562 ft. | 1,000 m. 3,281 ft. | 500 m. 1,640 ft. | 200 m. 656 ft. | 100 m. 328 ft. | Sea Level | Below

GLOSSARY OF ABBREVIATIONS

A
Afgh., Afghan. — Afghanistan
Afr. — Africa
Ala. — Alabama
Alb. — Albania
Alg. — Algeria
Alta. — Alberta
Amer. Samoa — American Samoa
arch. — archipelago
Arg. — Argentina
Ariz. — Arizona
Ark. — Arkansas
Arm. — Armenia
Aust., Austr. — Australia
Azer. — Azerbaijan

B
Bah. — Bahrain
Bang. — Bangladesh
Barb. — Barbados
Bel. — Belarus
Belg. — Belgium
Ben. — Benin
Bh. — Bhutan
Bol. — Bolivia
Bosn. — Bosnia and Herzegovina
Bots. — Botswana
Braz. — Brazil
Br. — British
Br. Ind. Oc. Terr. — British
  Indian Ocean Territory
Bulg. — Bulgaria

C
c. — cape
Calif. — California
Cam. — Cameroon
Camb. — Cambodia
cap. — capital
Cent. Afr. Rep. — Central African
  Republic
chan. — channel
Col. — Colombia
Colo. — Colorado
Conn. — Connecticut
C. R. — Costa Rica
Czech Rep. — Czech Republic

D
Del. — Delaware
Den. — Denmark
des. — desert
Dom. Rep. — Dominican Republic

E
Ec. — Ecuador
El Sal. — El Salvador
Eng. — England
Est. — Estonia
est. — estuary
Eth. — Ethiopia
Eur. — Europe

F
Fla. — Florida
Fr. — France, French
Fr. Gu. — French
  Guiana
Ft. — Fort
F.Y.R.O.M. — Former Yugoslav
  Republic of Macedonia

G
Ga. — Georgia (state)
Gamb. — Gambia
Geo. — Georgia (nation)
Ger. — Germany
Gr. — Greece
Gren. — Grenada
Guat. — Guatemala
Gui.-Bis. — Guinea-Bissau
Guy. — Guyana

H
Hond. — Honduras
Hung. — Hungary

I
i., isl. — island
Ice. — Iceland
Ill. — Illinois
Ind. — Indiana
Indon. — Indonesia
Ire. — Ireland
is., isls. — islands
Isr. — Israel
It. — Italy, Italian

J
Jam. — Jamaica
Jap. — Japan, Japanese
Jor. — Jordan

K
Kans. — Kansas
Kaz. — Kazakhstan
Ky. — Kentucky
Kyr. — Kyrgyzstan

L
l. — lake
La. — Louisiana
Lat. — Latvia
Liech. — Liechtenstein
Lith. — Lithuania
Lux. — Luxembourg

M
Mal. — Malawi
Man. — Manitoba
Mass. — Massachusetts
Maur. — Mauritania
Md. — Maryland
Mex. — Mexico
Mich. — Michigan
Minn. — Minnesota
Miss. — Mississippi
Mo. — Missouri
Mold. — Moldova
Mont. — Montana
Monte. — Montenegro
Mor. — Morocco
Moz. — Mozambique
mt., mte. — mount
mts. — mountains

N
N. Amer. — North America
nat'l — national
N. B. — New Brunswick
N. C. — North Carolina
N. Cal. — New Caledonia
N. Dak. — North Dakota
Nebr. — Nebraska
Neth. — Netherlands
Neth. Ant. — Netherlands Antilles
Nev. — Nevada
Newf. — Newfoundland
N. H. — New Hampshire
Nic. — Nicaragua
Nig. — Nigeria
N. Ire. — Northern Ireland
N. J. — New Jersey
N. Kor. — North Korea
N. Mex. — New Mexico
N. S. — Nova Scotia
N. S. W. — New South Wales
N. Terr. — Northern Territories
N. W. T. — Northwest Territories
N. Y. — New York
N. Z. — New Zealand

O
Okla. — Oklahoma
Ont. — Ontario
Oreg. — Oregon

P
Pa. — Pennsylvania
Pak. — Pakistan
Pan. — Panama
Par. — Paraguay
P. E. I. — Prince Edward Island

(continued)
pen. — peninsula
Phil. — Philippines
plat. — plateau
Pol. — Poland
Port. — Portugal, Portuguese
P. R. — Puerto Rico
pt. pte. — point

Q
Que. — Québec
Queens. — Queensland

R
r., riv. — river
ra. — range
reg. — region
rep. — republic
res. — reservoir
R. I. — Rhode Island
Rom. — Romania

S
sa. — sierra, serra
S. Afr. — South Africa
S. Amer. — South America
Sask. — Saskatchewan
S. Austr. — South Australia
Saudi Ar. — Saudi Arabia
S. C. — South Carolina
Scot. — Scotland
sd. — sound
S. Dak. — South Dakota
Sen. — Senegal
Serb. — Serbia
S.Kor. — South Korea
Sp. — Spain, Spanish
sprs. — springs
st., ste. — saint, sainte
sta. — station
str. — strait
Sur. — Suriname
Swaz. — Swaziland
Switz. — Switzerland
Syr. — Syria

T
Taj. — Tajikistan
Tan. — Tanzania
Tenn. — Tennessee
terr. — territory
Thai. — Thailand
Trin. & Tob. — Trinidad and
  Tobago
Trkm. — Turkmenistan
Tun. — Tunisia
Turk. — Turkey

U
U. A. E. — United Arab Emirates
U. K. — United Kingdom
Ukr. — Ukraine
un. — united
Urug. — Uruguay
U.S. — United States
Uzb. — Uzbekistan

V
Va. — Virginia
Ven. — Venezuela
Vic. — Victoria
vol. — volcano
Vt. — Vermont

W
Wash. — Washington
W. I. — West Indies
Wis. — Wisconsin
W. Va. — West Virginia
Wyo. — Wyoming

Z
Zim. — Zimbabwe

GAZETTEER-INDEX OF THE WORLD

Place	Area (Sq. Mi.)	Area (Sq. Km.)	Population	Page Ref.
*Afghanistan	250,775	649,507	31,889,923	61
Africa	11,707,000	30,321,130	910,850,000	33
Alabama, U.S.A.	52,423	135,775	4,447,100	15
Alaska, U.S.A.	656,424	1,700,139	626,932	20
*Albania	11,100	28,749	3,600,523	51
Alberta, Canada	255,285	661,185	3,064,249	11
*Algeria	919,591	2,381,740	33,333,216	35
*Andorra	188	487	71,822	47
*Angola	481,351	1,246,700	12,263,596	38
Antarctica	5,500,000	14,245,000	--------	72
*Antigua and Barbuda	171	443	69,481	24
*Argentina	1,072,070	2,776,661	40,301,927	31
Arizona, U.S.A.	114,006	295,276	5,130,632	19
Arkansas, U.S.A.	53,182	137,742	2,673,400	17
*Armenia	11,506	29,800	2,971,650	53
Asia	17,128,500	44,362,815	3,958,768,000	55
*Australia	2,966,136	7,682,300	20,434,176	68
*Austria	32,375	83,851	8,199,783	50
*Azerbaijan	33,436	86,600	8,120,247	53
*Bahamas	5,382	13,939	305,655	24
*Bahrain	240	622	708,573	57
*Bangladesh	55,126	142,776	150,448,339	61
*Barbados	166	430	280,946	24
*Belarus	80,154	207,600	9,724,723	53
*Belgium	11,781	30,513	10,392,226	45
*Belize	8,867	22,966	294,385	22
*Benin	43,483	112,620	8,078,314	35
Bermuda, U.K.	21	54	66,163	9
*Bhutan	18,147	47,000	2,327,849	61
*Bolivia	424,163	1,098,582	9,119,152	30
*Bosnia & Herzegovina	19,940	51,129	4,552,198	51
*Botswana	224,764	582,139	1,639,131	38
*Brazil	3,284,426	8,506,663	190,010,647	30
British Columbia, Canada	366,253	948,596	4,095,934	11
*Brunei	2,226	5,765	386,511	64
*Bulgaria	42,823	110,912	7,322,858	51
*Burkina Faso	105,869	274,200	14,326,203	35
*Burundi	10,747	27,835	8,390,505	37
California, U.S.A.	163,707	424,002	33,871,648	19
*Cambodia	69,898	181,036	14,131,858	65
*Cameroon	183,568	475,441	18,060,382	37
*Canada	3,851,787	9,976,139	33,390,141	11
*Cape Verde	1,557	4,033	423,613	33
*Central African Republic	242,000	626,780	4,369,038	37
Central America	197,480	511,475	40,497,360	22
*Chad	495,752	1,283,998	10,238,807	36
*Chile	292,257	756,946	16,284,741	31
*China, People's Rep. of	3,691,000	9,559,690	1,321,851,888	62
China, Republic of (Taiwan)	13,971	36,185	23,174,294	62
*Colombia	439,513	1,138,339	44,227,550	28
Colorado, U.S.A.	104,100	269,620	4,301,261	19
*Comoros	719	1,862	710,960	33
*Congo, Democratic Republic of the	905,063	2,344,113	64,606,759	37
*Congo, Republic of the	132,046	342,000	3,800,610	37
Connecticut, U.S.A.	5,544	14,358	3,405,565	13
*Costa Rica	19,575	50,700	4,133,884	22
*Côte d'Ivoire (Ivory Coast)	124,504	322,465	18,013,409	35
*Croatia	22,050	56,538	4,493,312	51
*Cuba	44,206	114,494	11,416,987	24
*Cyprus	3,473	8,995	788,457	58
*Czech Republic	30,449	78,863	10,228,744	50
Delaware, U.S.A.	2,489	6,447	783,600	14
*Denmark	16,629	43,069	5,468,120	43
District of Columbia, U.S.A.	68	177	572,059	14
*Djibouti	8,880	23,000	496,374	36
*Dominica	290	751	68,925	24
*Dominican Republic	18,704	48,443	9,365,818	24
East Timor	5,743	14,874	1,084,971	64
*Ecuador	109,483	283,561	13,755,680	29
*Egypt	386,659	1,001,447	80,264,543	36
*El Salvador	8,260	21,393	6,939,688	22
England, U.K.	50,516	130,836	49,138,831	42
*Equatorial Guinea	10,831	28,052	551,201	37
*Eritrea	45,410	117,600	4,906,585	36
*Estonia	17,413	45,100	1,315,912	53
*Ethiopia	426,366	1,104,300	76,511,887	36
Europe	4,057,000	10,507,630	729,240,000	40
*Fiji	7,055	18,272	918,675	70
*Finland	130,128	337,032	5,238,460	43
Florida, U.S.A.	65,758	170,313	15,982,378	15
*France	210,038	543,998	61,083,916	46
French Guiana	35,135	91,000	203,321	28
French Polynesia	1,544	4,000	278,633	70
*Gabon	103,346	267,666	1,454,867	37
*Gambia	4,127	10,689	1,688,359	35
Gaza Strip	139	360	1,482,405	59
*Georgia	26,911	69,700	4,646,003	53
Georgia, U.S.A.	59,441	153,953	8,186,453	15
*Germany	137,753	356,780	82,400,996	44
*Ghana	92,099	238,536	22,931,299	35
Gibraltar, U.K.	2.28	5.91	27,967	47
*Greece	50,944	131,945	10,706,290	51
Greenland, Den.	840,000	2,175,600	56,344	9
*Grenada	133	344	89,971	24
Guam, U.S.	209	541	173,456	70
*Guatemala	42,042	108,889	12,728,111	22
*Guinea	94,925	245,856	9,947,814	35
*Guinea-Bissau	13,948	36,125	1,472,041	35
*Guyana	83,000	214,970	769,095	28
*Haiti	10,694	27,697	8,706,497	24
Hawaii, U.S.A.	10,932	28,313	1,211,537	20
*Honduras	43,277	112,087	7,483,763	22
Hong Kong, China	403	1,044	6,980,412	62
*Hungary	35,919	93,030	9,956,108	50
*Iceland	39,768	103,000	301,931	43
Idaho, U.S.A.	83,574	216,456	1,293,953	18
Illinois, U.S.A.	57,918	150,007	12,419,293	16
*India	1,269,339	3,287,588	1,129,866,154	61
Indiana, U.S.A.	36,420	94,328	6,080,485	16
*Indonesia	788,430	2,042,034	234,693,997	64
Iowa, U.S.A.	56,276	145,754	2,926,324	16
*Iran	636,293	1,648,000	65,397,521	60
*Iraq	172,476	446,713	27,499,638	60
*Ireland	27,136	70,282	4,109,086	42
*Israel	7,847	20,324	6,426,679	59
*Italy	116,303	301,225	58,147,733	48
*Jamaica	4,411	11,424	2,780,132	24
*Japan	145,730	377,441	127,467,972	63
*Jordan	35,000	90,650	6,053,193	59
Kansas, U.S.A.	82,282	213,110	2,688,418	16
*Kazakhstan	1,048,300	2,715,100	15,284,929	53
Kentucky, U.S.A.	40,411	104,665	4,041,769	15
*Kenya	224,960	582,646	36,913,721	37
Kiribati	291	754	107,817	70
*Korea, North	46,540	120,539	23,301,725	63
*Korea, South	38,175	98,873	49,044,790	63
*Kuwait	6,532	16,918	2,505,559	57
*Kyrgyzstan	76,641	198,500	5,284,149	53
*Laos	91,428	236,800	6,521,998	65
*Latvia	24,595	63,700	2,259,810	53
*Lebanon	4,015	10,399	3,921,278	58
*Lesotho	11,720	30,355	2,012,649	38
*Liberia	43,000	111,370	3,193,942	35
*Libya	679,358	1,759,537	6,036,914	36
*Liechtenstein	61	158	34,247	49
*Lithuania	25,174	65,200	3,575,439	53
Louisiana, U.S.A.	51,843	134,275	4,468,976	17
*Luxembourg	999	2,587	480,222	45
Macau, China	11	28	480,222	62
*Macedonia (F.Y.R.O.M.)	9,889	25,713	2,055,915	51
*Madagascar	226,657	587,041	19,448,815	38
Maine, U.S.A.	35,387	91,653	1,274,923	13
*Malawi	45,747	118,485	13,603,181	38
Malaya, Malaysia	50,806	131,588	18,523,632	65
*Malaysia	128,308	332,318	24,821,286	64
*Maldives	115	298	369,031	55

Place	Area (Sq. Mi.)	Area (Sq. Km.)	Population	Page Ref.
*Mali	464,873	1,204,021	11,995,402	35
*Malta	122	316	401,880	48
Manitoba, Canada	250,999	650,087	1,150,034	11
*Marshall Islands	70	181	61,782	70
Maryland, U.S.A.	12,407	32,135	5,296,486	14
Massachusetts, U.S.A.	10,555	27,337	6,349,097	13
*Mauritania	419,229	1,085,803	3,270,065	35
*Mauritius	790	2,046	1,250,882	55
*Mexico	761,601	1,972,546	108,700,891	21
Michigan, U.S.A.	96,810	250,738	9,938,444	16
*Micronesia, Fed. States of...	271	702	107,862	70
Minnesota, U.S.A.	86,943	225,182	4,919,479	16
Mississippi, U.S.A.	48,434	125,443	2,844,658	15
Missouri, U.S.A.	69,709	180,546	5,595,211	16
*Moldova	13,012	33,700	4,320,490	53
*Monaco	368 acres	149 ha.	32,671	46
*Mongolia	606,163	1,569,962	2,874,127	62
Montana, U.S.A.	147,046	380,850	902,195	18
*Montenegro	5,333	13,812	684,736	51
*Morocco	172,414	446,550	33,757,175	35
*Mozambique	303,769	786,762	20,905,585	38
*Myanmar (Burma)	261,789	678,034	47,373,958	65
*Namibia	317,827	823,172	2,055,080	38
Nauru	7.7	20	13,528	70
Nebraska, U.S.A.	82,282	213,110	1,711,263	16
*Nepal	54,663	141,577	28,901,790	61
*Netherlands	15,892	41,160	16,570,613	45
Nevada, U.S.A.	110,567	286,368	1,998,257	19
New Brunswick, Canada	28,354	73,437	757,077	11
Newfoundland, Canada	156,184	404,517	533,761	11
New Hampshire, U.S.A.	9,351	24,219	1,235,786	13
New Jersey, U.S.A.	8,722	22,590	8,414,350	14
New Mexico, U.S.A.	121,598	314,939	1,819,046	19
New York, U.S.A.	54,475	141,089	18,976,457	14
*New Zealand	103,736	268,676	4,115,771	68
*Nicaragua	45,698	118,358	5,675,356	22
*Niger	489,189	1,267,000	12,894,865	35
*Nigeria	357,000	924,630	135,031,164	35
North America	9,363,000	24,250,170	517,856,000	9
North Carolina, U.S.A.	53,821	139,397	8,049,313	15
North Dakota, U.S.A.	70,704	183,123	642,200	16
Northern Ireland, U.K.	5,452	14,121	1,685,267	42
Northwest Territories, Canada	1,304,896	3,379,683	40,860	11
*Norway	125,053	323,887	4,627,926	43
Nova Scotia, Canada	21,425	55,491	942,691	11
Nunavut, Canada	733,590	1,900,000	28,159	11
Ohio, U.S.A.	44,828	116,103	11,353,140	16
Oklahoma, U.S.A.	69,903	181,049	3,450,654	17
*Oman	120,000	310,800	3,204,897	57
Ontario, Canada	412,580	1,068,582	11,874,436	11
Oregon, U.S.A.	98,386	254,819	3,421,399	18
*Pakistan	310,403	803,944	169,270,617	61
*Palau	188	487	20,842	70
*Panama	29,761	77,082	3,242,173	22
*Papua New Guinea	183,540	475,369	5,795,887	64
*Paraguay	157,047	406,752	6,667,147	31
Pennsylvania, U.S.A.	46,058	119,291	12,281,054	14
*Peru	496,222	1,285,215	28,674,757	29
*Philippines	115,707	299,681	91,077,287	66
*Poland	120,725	312,678	38,518,241	52
*Portugal	35,549	92,072	10,642,836	47
Prince Edward Island, Canada	2,184	5,657	138,514	11
Puerto Rico, U.S.	3,515	9,104	3,944,259	24
*Qatar	4,247	11,000	907,229	57
Québec, Canada	594,857	1,540,680	7,410,504	11
Rhode Island, U.S.A.	1,545	4,002	1,048,319	13
*Romania	91,699	237,500	22,276,056	51
*Russia	6,592,812	17,075,400	141,377,752	53
*Rwanda	10,169	26,337	9,907,509	37
*Saint Kitts and Nevis	104	269	39,349	24
*Saint Lucia	238	616	170,649	24
*Saint Vincent & the Grenadines	150	388	118,149	24
*Samoa	1,133	2,934	176,615	70
*San Marino	23.4	60.6	29,615	48
*São Tomé and Príncipe	372	963	199,579	35
Saskatchewan, Canada	251,699	651,900	1,015,783	11
*Saudi Arabia	829,995	2,149,687	27,601,038	57
Scotland, U.K.	30,414	78,772	5,062,011	42
*Senegal	75,954	196,720	12,521,851	35
*Serbia	34,185	88,538	10,150,265	51
*Seychelles	145	375	81,895	55
*Sierra Leone	27,925	72,325	6,144,562	35
*Singapore	226	585	4,553,009	65
*Slovakia	18,924	49,014	5,447,502	50
*Slovenia	7,898	20,251	2,009,245	51
*Solomon Islands	11,500	29,785	566,842	70
*Somalia	246,200	637,658	9,118,773	37
*South Africa	455,318	1,179,274	43,997,828	38
South America	6,875,000	17,806,250	375,641,000	26
South Carolina, U.S.A.	32,007	82,898	4,012,012	15
South Dakota, U.S.A.	77,358	200,358	754,844	16
*Spain	194,881	504,742	40,448,191	47
*Sri Lanka	25,332	65,610	20,926,315	61
*Sudan	967,494	2,505,809	42,292,929	36
*Suriname	55,144	142,823	470,784	28
*Swaziland	6,705	17,366	1,133,066	38
*Sweden	173,665	449,792	9,031,088	43
Switzerland	15,943	41,292	7,554,661	49
*Syria	71,498	185,180	19,314,747	58
Taiwan	13,971	36,185	23,174,294	62
*Tajikistan	55,251	143,100	7,076,598	53
*Tanzania	363,708	942,003	38,139,640	37
Tennessee, U.S.A.	42,146	109,158	5,689,283	15
Texas, U.S.A.	268,601	695,676	20,851,820	17
*Thailand	198,455	513,998	65,068,149	65
*Togo	21,622	56,000	5,701,579	35
Tonga	270	699	116,921	70
*Trinidad and Tobago	1,980	5,128	1,056,608	24
*Tunisia	63,378	164,149	10,276,158	35
*Turkey	300,946	779,450	71,158,647	58
*Turkmenistan	188,455	488,100	5,136,262	53
Tuvalu	9.78	25.33	11,992	70
*Uganda	91,076	235,887	30,262,610	37
*Ukraine	233,089	603,700	46,299,862	53
*United Arab Emirates	32,278	83,600	2,642,566	57
*United Kingdom	94,399	244,493	60,776,238	42
*United States of America	3,536,338	9,159,116	301,139,947	12
*Uruguay	72,172	186,925	3,447,496	31
Utah, U.S.A.	84,904	219,902	2,233,169	19
*Uzbekistan	173,591	449,600	27,780,059	53
*Vanuatu	5,700	14,763	211,971	70
Vatican City	108.7 acres	44 ha.	921	48
*Venezuela	352,143	912,050	26,084,662	28
Vermont, U.S.A.	9,615	24,903	608,827	13
*Vietnam	128,405	332,569	85,262,356	65
Virginia, U.S.A.	42,769	110,771	7,078,515	15
Virgin Islands, U.K.	59	153	23,552	24
Virgin Islands, U.S.A.	132	342	108,448	24
Wales, U.K.	8,017	20,764	2,903,085	42
Washington, U.S.A.	71,303	184,674	5,894,121	18
West Bank	2,263	5,860	2,535,927	59
Western Sahara	102,703	266,000	382,617	35
West Virginia, U.S.A.	24,231	62,759	1,808,344	15
Wisconsin, U.S.A.	65,503	169,653	5,363,675	16
World (land)	57,970,000	150,142,300	6,525,487,000	3
Wyoming, U.S.A.	97,818	253,349	493,782	18
*Yemen	188,321	487,752	22,211,743	57
Yukon Territory, Canada	207,075	536,324	29,885	11
*Zambia	290,586	752,618	11,477,447	38
*Zimbabwe	150,803	390,580	12,311,143	38

* Member of the United Nations

INDEX OF THE WORLD

GLOSSARY OF GEOGRAPHICAL TERMS

altitude — a height above sea level.

Antarctic Circle — an imaginary line of latitude 66° 30′ (66 degrees 30 minutes) south of the Equator. On June 21 the sun does not rise along the Circle and on Dec. 22 it does not set.

archipelago — a group or chain of islands.

Arctic Circle — an imaginary line of latitude 66° 30′ (66 degrees 30 minutes) north of the Equator. On Dec. 22 the sun does not rise along the Circle and on June 21 it does not set.

atoll — a coral reef surrounding a central lagoon.

basin — 1) a land area surrounded by higher borderlands, or 2) the entire area drained by a river and its branches.

bay — a branch of the sea indenting the land, generally with a wide opening, but usually more narrow than a gulf.

canal — a narrow, man-made channel of water joining lakes or rivers, or connecting them with the sea, and used for navigation or irrigation.

canyon — a deep, narrow valley.

cape (or point) — a piece of land extending into the water.

channel — 1) a narrow passage of water, but wider than a strait, connecting two large bodies of water, or 2) the deepest part of a river or harbor.

continent — one of the large, continuous areas of the earth into which the land surface is divided.

degree — a unit of measurement of a circle, represented by the symbol °. There are 180° of latitude, 90° north of the Equator to the North Pole and 90° south of the Equator to the South Pole. 360° of longitude circle the earth, stretching 180° in either direction from the Prime Meridian of Greenwich. Degrees are subdivided into 60 minutes, represented by the symbol ′.

delta — a low, usually fan-shaped area of alluvial land at a river's mouth.

depression — a low land area, often below sea level, without drainage outlet.

desert — a barren land area so dry as to support little or no vegetation.

Eastern Hemisphere — the half of the global sphere that embraces Europe, Asia, Africa, and Australia, and their waters; also called the "Old World."

Equator — an imaginary line of latitude (0°) midway between the two poles.

estuary — a branch of the ocean at the mouth of a large river, which is affected by ocean tides as well as the flow of the river.

fall — a sudden drop of a river from a high level to a much lower one.

fjord (or fiord) — a long narrow inlet or arm of the ocean bordered by high cliffs.

forest — a large area of land densely covered with trees and underbrush.

glacier — a large mass of ice that moves slowly down a valley from highlands toward sea level.

gulf — a branch of the ocean indenting the land.

highland — an elevated area of land with irregular base levels, but generally with fairly even heights.

hill — a slightly elevated point of land rising above its surroundings.

ice shelf — a thick mass of ice extending from a polar shore. The seaward edge is afloat and sometimes extends hundreds of miles out to sea.

International Date Line — an imaginary line of longitude generally 180° east or west of the Prime Meridian, along which the date changes by one day. Going west, for instance, the moment at which one crosses the Date Line becomes the corresponding moment of the following day.

island — an area of land completely surrounded by water.

isthmus — a narrow strip of land located between two bodies of water, and connecting two larger bodies of land.

key (or cay) — 1) a low island, usually composed of sand, or 2) a reef.

lagoon — a shallow area of water separated from the ocean by a sand bank or by a strip of low land.

lake — an area of fresh or salt water entirely surrounded by land.

latitude — distance measured in degrees north or south of the Equator.

longitude — the distance measured in degrees east or west of the Prime Meridian.

massif — a compact mass of high elevations with sharply defined borders.

meridian — an imaginary line of longitude running between two poles.

mountain — an unusually high elevation rising steeply above its surroundings.

North Pole — the northern extremity of the earth, 90° north of the Equator.

North Tropic Line (or Tropic of Cancer) — an imaginary line of latitude 23° 30′ north of the Equator. It is the most northerly position at which the sun's rays fall vertically on the earth (only June 21).

oasis — a desert area made fertile by the presence of water.

ocean — one of the large, continuous areas of the earth into which the water surface is divided.

parallel — latitude lines running east and west parallel to the Equator.

peak — 1) the highest point of a mountain, or 2) a mountain that has a pointed top.

peninsula — an area of land extending into the sea, surrounded by water on three sides.

plain — a flat or a level area of land.

plateau (or tableland) — a highland plain, or elevated area of generally level land, sometimes containing deep canyons.

Prime Meridian — the starting point (0°) passing through Greenwich, England, for the lines of longitude running east and west.

range (or mountain range) — a connecting chain of high elevations.

reef — a chain of rocks, sand or coral usually just below sea level, but often with dry areas above the surface.

reservoir — a man-made lake in which water is collected and stored for use. The amount of water is controlled by a *dam*.

river — a stream of water larger than a creek, generally flowing to another stream, a lake, or to the ocean.

scale — the relationship of the length between two points as shown on a map and the true distance between the two points on the earth.

sea — a large area of salt water smaller than an ocean, sometimes occurring within a land area with no outlet to the ocean.

sound — a body of water connecting two larger bodies of water, generally wider than a channel or strait.

South Pole — the southern extremity of the earth, 90° south of the Equator.

South Tropic Line (or Tropic of Capricorn) — an imaginary line of latitude 23° 30′ south of the Equator. It is the most southerly position at which the sun's rays fall vertically on the earth (only Dec. 21).

strait — a narrow body of water connecting two larger bodies of water.

swamp — a low area of wet, spongy ground, usually containing reed-like vegetation.

valley — a long hollow, usually with an outlet, lying between two areas of higher elevation, and generally containing a stream.

volcano — a mountain that has (active) or had (inactive) openings in the earth's crust from which lava escapes, making it more or less cone-shaped.

Western Hemisphere — the half of the global sphere that embraces North and South America and their waters; also called the "New World".